Performance Management

Harvard Business Essentials

The New Manager's Guide and Mentor

The Harvard Business Essentials series is designed to provide comprehensive advice, personal coaching, background information, and guidance on the most relevant topics in business. Drawing on rich content from Harvard Business School Publishing and other sources, these concise guides are carefully crafted to provide a highly practical resource for readers with all levels of experience, and will prove especially valuable for the new manager. To assure quality and accuracy, each volume is closely reviewed by a specialized content adviser from a world-class business school. Whether you are a new manager seeking to expand your skills or a seasoned professional looking to broaden your knowledge base, these solution-oriented books put reliable answers at your fingertips.

Other books in the series:

HARVARD
BUSINESS
ESSENTIALS

Performance Management

*Measure and Improve the
Effectiveness of Your Employees*

Harvard Business School Press | *Boston, Massachusetts*

978-1-59139-842-4 (ISBN 13)
Library of Congress Cataloging-in-Publication Data
Harvard business essentials : performance management : measure and improve
the effectiveness of your employees.
p. cm. — (Harvard business essentials series)
Includes bibliographical references.
ISBN 1-59139-842-8
1. Personnel management. 2. Performance standards. I. Harvard Business School.
II. Series: Harvard business essentials series.
HF5549.P4175 2006
658.3'125—dc22
2006006678

Contents

Performance Management

Introduction

When you look at your workforce, do you see the source of your organization's success? Are the human resources at your disposal competent and committed to key company goals? Are your subordinates skillful and motivated to beat the competition? Is their work getting better over time?

If you answered yes to these questions, your unit or company is positioned for success. If you answered no to any of them, you could benefit from performance management. *Performance management* is a method used to measure and improve the effectiveness of people in the workplace. If you are an executive or a manager, performance management is a core skill, one that you can use throughout your career. Performance management is actually a system composed of several activities, including goal setting, tracking changes, coaching, motivation, appraisal (or review), and employee development. Figure I-1 indicates how these activities, which involve managers and their employees, are variously cyclic and ongoing.

The performance management cycle, as it is commonly understood, begins with goal setting. Performance is then tracked against the employee's goals and eventually appraised, usually in a formal year-end meeting. An informal midyear review is generally recommended. The results of the formal appraisal feed into the organization's rewards system of pay and bonuses and are used in decisions regarding promotion and retention. Also, depending on the results of the appraisal, the manager and employee may agree on a plan of skill or career development aimed at expanding the individual's capabilities and contribution to the company. And then the cycle begins anew, with a reevaluation of the employee's goals.

FIGURE I-1

The performance management system

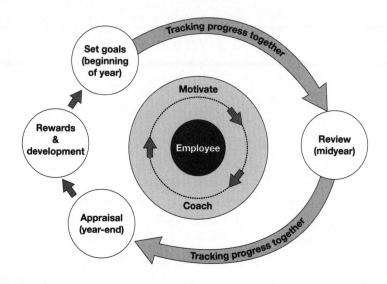

Source: Adapted with permission from Brian J. Hall.

This tidy, step-by-step cycle represents only one aspect of performance management. The other—motivating and coaching by the manager—does not fit into a linear progression. Motivating and coaching have no seasons. They are either ongoing or applied as needed.

Why Performance Management Matters

Competitiveness in many of today's industries is based on the effectiveness of human assets—on the ability of employees to create, to apply their skills and accumulated knowledge, to work effectively together, and to treat customers well. Yes, physical and financial assets are often essential, but in many instances, creativity and human resourcefulness are more important as "differentiators" and as sources of long-term competitive advantage. Perhaps this is the case in your industry.

The importance of human assets in business competition explains why every company and every manager needs a system for making the most of the company's people resources. Everyone benefits when an organization has effective performance management:

- Shareholders observe better results, because the human assets of the organization are top-notch and working in unison toward key goals.

- Managers are more successful, because their subordinates are doing the right things well.

- Employees experience greater job security, career advancement, and fatter paychecks, thanks to outstanding performance.

What's Ahead

Harvard Business Essentials: Performance Management can help you improve the effectiveness of the people who work for you. The literature on employee performance is large and growing constantly, with dozens of books and hundreds of articles and case studies published every year. This book presents some of the best of that information in a practical format that you can apply today. It provides essential ideas on employee performance, with many examples drawn from the contemporary business scene, and with practical tips to make your efforts more effective.

If performance management were a purely linear process (do this, then do that, and then . . .), organizing this book would have be simple. But some aspects of the subject don't follow a strictly linear process. So, we've arranged the topics in a chapter order that proceeds roughly in the way a manager would deal with employee performance, beginning with the indisputable starting point: goal setting. Chapter 1 explains the importance of goals and the characteristics that effective goals share. It goes on to describe the importance of goal alignment throughout the organization. If individual employee goals aren't aligned with unit and company goals, you'll have big trouble.

Chapter 2 is a short primer on motivation—something managers must attend to *all the time*. If you want people to pursue their assigned goals, you must make sure that they are sufficiently motivated to do so. Here we provide a brief overview of the classic theories of motivation and the intrinsic and extrinsic rewards you can use to encourage people to do their best. In reading this chapter, you will find practical techniques you can use to motivate your subordinates.

With your employees in pursuit of their goals, it's smart to monitor progress periodically. Regular progress checks provide opportunities to remind employees about goals and the importance of those goals, give you a chance to offer positive feedback about the good things that your employees are doing, and help you spot small problems before they become large ones. Chapter 3 gives you a practical method for objectively monitoring performance and catching those problems. It also includes a short section on the common sources of performance problems.

Beginning managers don't think of themselves as coaches. Most were taught that managers do four things: plan, direct, motivate, and control. "Our textbook didn't say anything about coaching!" But experienced managers recognize that coaching is a big part of their jobs. They use coaching to close performance gaps, teach skills, impart knowledge, motivate, and inculcate desirable work behaviors. Good managers are always looking for coaching opportunities.

Coaching is so important that we devote two chapters to it. Chapter 4 covers the basics with a four-step process you can begin using right away. Chapter 5 goes beyond the basics to explain how you can safely delegate some coaching responsibilities to others. Doing that will save you time and give your surrogate coach an opportunity to hone a skill he or she may need someday as a manager. The chapter describes three conditions that improve coaching results. And it illustrates common mistakes made by coaches—and the remedies for those mistakes.

Many companies today require an annual performance appraisal for each employee. Chances are that you have been on both sides of this technique: as appraiser and as "appraisee." Chapter 6 explains the role of appraisal in the larger system of performance manage-

ment and offers an eight-step process for doing it well. We also describe 360-degree feedback, a technique that reports on a person's
work effectiveness from more perspectives than just the boss's.

A formal performance appraisal typically feeds into the company's pay and promotions schemes. It also identifies opportunities
for enhancing the skills and careers of people who want to step up to
new challenges or greater responsibility. We cover the issue of employee development in chapter 7. There, you'll find a brief discussion of why employee development is an important part of every
manager's job. We follow the discussion with four practical approaches you can take to help people enhance their skills and careers.

We've titled chapter 8 "Intractable Performance Problems." If
you've been managing for a while, you've surely run into some of
these challenges: people who simply aren't doing the job well and
aren't motivated to improve. Then there are the people who try, but
who can't get it right. How do you handle these cases? We approach
these employees through problem diagnosis followed by confrontation, with feedback. The chapter goes on to offer specific advice for
dealing with C-level performers, burnout cases, and people for
whom dismissal is the best solution.

Because this is an "essentials" book, we've had to be very selective
with our topics. There is more to managing performance than what's
covered in these chapters. Readers who want to learn more should
refer to the "For Further Reading" section at the end of the book.
There, we've listed several useful articles and books that can add
greatly to your understanding of employee performance management.
We've also included a glossary of key terms to enhance learning.
Performance management uses a number of unique terms: 360-
degree feedback, intrinsic and extrinsic rewards, and career ladders,
to name just a few. We have italicized these important terms in the
text. That's your cue that their definitions can be found in the end-
of-book glossary.

We've also provided two appendices. The first one contains
several useful items, including a coach's self-evaluation checklist,

which was first developed for our online publication Harvard ManageMentor. This self-diagnosis will help you understand your strengths and weaknesses as a coach. You can download a copy of this checklist from the Harvard Business Essentials series Web site, at www.elearning.hbsp.org/businesstools. While you're on that site, check out the online tools associated with other books in the series; you may find several of these tools useful in your work.

The other item in appendix A is an annual performance appraisal form. If your company doesn't have appraisal guidelines, you can adapt this one to your needs.

Finally, appendix B contains a primer entitled "Handling a Dismissal." This item will steer you past some of the land mines involved in dismissing a nonperforming employee.

We wish you every success in your management career.

Goals

Guides to Action

Key Topics Covered in This Chapter

- *Formulating goals*

- *Getting alignment*

- *The characteristics of effective goals*

- *Planning for success*

PERFORMANCE MANAGEMENT begins with goals. Goals define the results that people should aim to achieve. Goals are touchstones for performance planning, appraisal, rewards, and improvement. Without goals, time and energy would be wasted on activities that contribute very little to organizational success.

Every company, every operating unit, and every employee needs goals and plans for achieving them. Goals focus the limited resources and time of individuals and organizations on the things that matter most. Some goals must also be shared. Without shared goals, people would strike out in different directions and collaboration would be minimal.

If goals are so important, then who determines them? Setting goals is one of the essential functions of management. As a manager, you are responsible for setting goals for your unit and for each of its members. You must also work with others to create plans that people can follow in reaching their goals.

This chapter describes the characteristics of effective goals. It explains how to avoid mistakes in structuring goals and how to align goals throughout the organization. It also provides steps that you and your subordinates can take to assure that goals are attained.

Goals Begin at the Top—Well, Almost

From a purely logical perspective, goal setting should be a top-down process that begins in company strategy. If, for example, the strategic goal is to become the market share leader through rapid product introductions, then unit goals should serve that strategy. And individual goals should be aligned with those of their units. There should be, in fact, a cascading of linked and aligned goals from the top of the organization to the bottom, as described in figure 1-1. In this figure, the enterprise's strategic goal is at the top. Each of the operating units has goals that directly support the strategic objective. Within the operating units, teams and individuals are assigned goals that directly support the goals of their units.

The real power of these cascading goals is their alignment with the highest purposes of the organization. Every employee in this arrangement should understand his or her goals, how assigned activities advance the goals of the unit, and how the unit's activities contribute to the strategic objective of the enterprise. Thus, goal alignment focuses all the energy of the business on the things that matter most.

One warning: goal setting—at the top and at lower levels—is not as strictly top-down as we've described. Nor should it be. Dictating goals from on high is not practical, because doing so would fail

FIGURE 1-1

Goal alignment from top to bottom

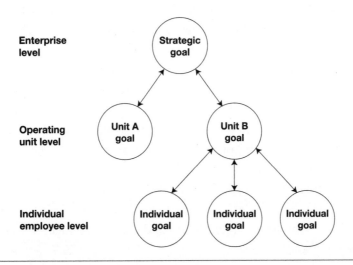

to recognize the interests and potential contributions of people up and down the organizational ladder. Consider the starting point of goals: top-level strategy. No experienced CEO trusts himself or herself to think of and dictate the best possible strategy. Instead, a smart executive enlists the ideas and suggestions of others: the top management team, division heads, technical experts at lower levels, and so forth. Together, these people argue the merits of many alternative courses of action, and in the process, the personal goals of many people are reflected in the company's strategy. Only by consulting with others in this way can the CEO appreciate the rewards and risks of various alternatives. Only by understanding the company's employees can a chief executive assess their abilities and willingness to execute a given strategy. A CEO must find ways for their voices to enter the strategy-setting process.

The same idea sharing and negotiating should take place at lower levels—though perhaps less so at the lowest levels. For example, suppose that the company's strategic goal is to increase market share through rapid new-product introductions. As the head of new-product development, you would not simply tell your people to increase new-product launches by some percentage that you determined. Instead, you would confer with your direct reports and marketing personnel about the best approach to fulfilling that strategy. Should your company crank out derivative versions of its most popular current products? If so, which ones? Should you leverage your core technologies to serve totally new users and uses?

In the end, the individual employee's goals must usually be represented in the formulation of unit goals. The alternative is for the boss to dictate goals to subordinates. But dictated goals are unlikely to inspire the kind of effort and creativity that produces good results. Goals that are negotiated with employees, in contrast, give those employees an important sense of goal ownership. And people are naturally more committed to the things they own. So, involve your employees in the goal-setting process. That way, you can be sure that (1) they have the capacity to assume responsibility for goals and (2) they understand the details and the importance of their assigned goals.

When Personal and Unit Goals Conflict

Every so often, you'll have a subordinate who doesn't think that a unit goal is very important—at least not to him or her. For example, a sales manager may have a new field sales representative whose personal goal is a job in market research. The rep is only in sales to build a résumé—period. People who cannot or will not get behind important goals belong somewhere else. But reasonable people can usually be persuaded to bite the bullet and give these goals their best shot. If you were the sales manager, what would you tell this field representative?

Thus, goal setting—both at the top level and at lower levels—should include a fair amount of give-and-take. This give-and-take works best when managers truly understand the people who work for them—and with them. What are the employees' personal ambitions? Are their personal goals compatible with the goals the unit must pursue? How can the unit goals be crafted to enlist the highest level of enthusiasm and support from subordinates?

Understanding your direct reports at a personal level will help you with goal setting. More important, it will help you with *every* facet of performance management. By understanding your subordinates, you'll have a better idea of how to motivate them. You'll know which rewards hit your people's hot buttons. (See "When Personal and Unit Goals Conflict" for a discussion about when your employees' aspirations don't match up with unit goals.) And you will be able to identify weaknesses that can be corrected through coaching or training.

Goals Versus Activities

It's very easy to confuse goals with activities. Activities describe how people spend their time, whereas goals are the results people seek.

Confusing the two can result in lots of well-intentioned activity but few positive results. Consider these examples:

Activities	Goals
Writing weekly sales report	Increase sales by 10 percent
Handling customer complaints and other problems	Reduce customer turnover by 15 percent
Meeting weekly to discuss new-product-development project	Launch five new products this year
Participating in quality-control training program	Cut production waste by 20 percent

Attempting to formulate goals through the employee's job description is sometimes the source of this confusion. A job description is a profile of a job and its essential functions, reporting relationships, level of authority, hours, and required credentials. The description is more about the content of the job than about the goals that managers and their subordinates agree to pursue. Consider this job description:

> As the executive assistant to the director, he or she will plan, schedule, and coordinate meetings of the director; record and transcribe meeting minutes; manage and track communications (phone, fax, and e-mail) by providing timely responses and distributing messages; assist in drafting, editing, copying, and distributing project reports and other materials; handle travel arrangements; assist with expense documentation and reimbursements; manage complicated schedules and day-to-day office systems; and perform other job-related duties as required. In addition, answering the office's phone will be required, as will various other clerical duties.

There are lots of activities listed in this job description, but no identifiable goals. As this example shows, you cannot use the job description as a substitute for defining a subordinate's goals.

Characteristics of Effective Goals

If goals are necessary, what are the characteristics of effective goals? Most experts agree that goals must be

- Recognized as important

- Clear

- Written in specific terms

- Measurable and framed in time

- Aligned with organizational strategy

- Achievable but challenging

- Supported by appropriate rewards

How do the goals of your employees stack up against this set of characteristics?

Perhaps a disclaimer about the required specificity of goals is appropriate here. In practice, goals for people at higher levels of responsibility tend to be more general, while goals for people at lower levels—people who have less discretion over their activities—tend to be more specified. Thus, at the top, we have the example of the directive issued to Admiral Ray Spruance by the U.S. Naval Command in the Pacific on the eve of the fateful Battle of Midway in June 1942: "Be governed by the principle of calculated risk, which you shall interpret to mean the avoidance of exposure of your force to superior enemy forces without good prospect of inflicting greater damage on the enemy."[1] There are no specifics in this directive. Naval Command left the details to Spruance to figure out as the situation unfolded.

The specificity of goals generally becomes greater as we go down to lower levels, where employees have less experience and need more direction. Consider this hypothetical example of a sales manager assigning goals to a field salesperson:

> *It's very important that our company increase its sales revenues during the coming calendar year. We've made sizable investments in training and manufacturing lately, and senior management expects us to cover those investments with higher revenues. If we can do that, the company's financial situation will be greatly improved and the company will be in a better competitive position for the future. And that means more job security and higher bonuses for everybody.*

The company's goal is to increase sales revenues by $15 million over the coming year, and everyone in the sales force is expected to contribute to that goal. Based on our discussions, your piece of the goal is to increase sales in your territory from $2 million to $2.2 million for the year—a 10 percent increase. I'll follow up with a written statement to that effect.

A 10 percent increase won't be easy, given the outstanding job you've done already, but there's still plenty of opportunity for growth in your territory. I'm confident that you can achieve that goal, and I'll back you up in any way I can.

Here, goals are very specific. Notice, too, how this manager touched on every characteristic of effective goals. He stated the goal in concrete terms and within a measurable time frame, explaining why it was important and how it aligned with company goals. He also promised to provide a written statement of the goals and told his subordinate about the benefits that would accrue to everyone if the goals were met.

Three Mistakes to Avoid

Many organizations make three mistakes in setting goals: (1) companies fail to create performance metrics, (2) they fail to align rewards with company and unit goals, and (3) the achievement bar is set too low. All three can undermine the value of goal setting.

Performance Metrics

Performance metrics provide objective evidence of goal achievement—or progress toward it. Sales revenues, output per machine, errors per thousand units of product, and time to market for new products are all examples of performance metrics. Whichever metrics you use, be sure that they are linked to your goals.

Some jobs involve goals and work for which performance metrics are difficult to create. If the goal is to increase revenues, it is quite easy to formulate quantitative, measurable metrics for the sales staff. For example, you may assign a sales quota: a 10 percent sales increase, or a sales goal of $2.2 million. But how do you create a performance metric for goals that are not easy to quantify, such as improving customer relations? Measuring customer relations may be infeasible. You may, however, be able to measure many things that contribute to improved customer relations, such as the number of customer complaints handled satisfactorily during a quarter or the average time required to resolve a customer problem.

So, don't assume that qualitative goals cannot be assigned performance metrics. (See "Soft Goals" for more discussion of metrics that are difficult to quantify.)

Goal and Reward Misalignments

Rewards are a facet of performance management that aims to encourage a particular behavior or outcome. They include anything that employees value: pay increases, bonuses, promotions, plumb assignments, and even travel junkets. Rewards should be aligned with goals, but that is easier said than done, since employees find ways to "game" even thoughtful reward systems.

Many companies change their goals but do not follow up with a realignment of rewards. Even when they try, companies often get it wrong and end up rewarding the wrong things. Worse, they may reward contradictory practices. For example, consultants Haig Nalbantian, Richard Guzzo, Dave Kieffer, and Jay Doherty cite the case of a U.S. manufacturer whose goal was to raise product quality.[2] This was goal number one for the company. Yet despite much effort, quality continued to slip. The cause of poor quality, this company discovered after much study, could be traced to a less explicit goal of giving young, promising managers broad experience by moving them between assignments every two years. This practice, in fact, was how managers moved up the ladder and received higher salaries. Those ambitious managers quickly learned that frequent movement was the best guarantor of pay increases and, ultimately, higher-level jobs.

Soft Goals

Some jobs involve important activities whose results are difficult to measure. For example, a young investment banker may be building customer relationships that will take years to pay off. A marketing specialist may write a plan for a new product line, but it will never be clear if the success or failure of the line resulted from the execution of her plan or the quality of the products. Many people call the goals associated with these hard-to-measure activities "soft" goals. Moreover, people often dismiss as marginally important whatever they can't measure. Don't make this mistake. Just because something is difficult to measure does not mean that it is unimportant. For example, the customer relationships being developed by the aforementioned young banker may be his employer's best assurance of a future stream of business.

Writing in *Harvard Management Update,* Karen Carney cites three keys to performance measurement for jobs that involve so-called soft goals:[a]

1. Involve people in determining their own performance criteria. Give people a list of company or unit goals, and ask which they can influence. Have them brainstorm about how they can help their internal or external customers.

2. Find qualified judges to assess people's performance according to these criteria. Judges may be fellow employees, customers, suppliers, or anyone else in a position to determine if results or behaviors meet, exceed, or fall short of expectations.

3. Combine hard and soft metrics as appropriate. One company cited by Carney bases bonuses on unit bottom-line results (a hard metric) and salary and promotion rewards on how fully each employee embodies the company's core values (soft metrics such as customer service and "does the right thing").

[a] Adapted from Karen Carney, "Successful Performance Appraisal: A Checklist," *Harvard Management Update,* November 1999, 4–5.

Unfortunately, rapid movement between assignments hurt product quality. The management of long-term product-development projects was being handed off every two years. The manager who started a project knew that he or she would be long gone—and not accountable for results—when the product eventually hit the market. Staying with a project from start to finish would impede a person's managerial career. In this case, misaligned rewards encouraged managers to put their energy into the wrong activities—moving from assignment to assignment—frustrating the company's goal of improving product quality.

Your best defense in cases like this one is to take a systems approach to goals and rewards. A systems approach can help you avoid the unintended consequences experienced by the manufacturer just described. (We'll have more on performance measurement and rewards in chapter 2, which covers motivation.)

Insufficient Challenge

Many managers are apprehensive in their approach to goal setting. On the one hand, they know that goals should address the most important challenges facing their organizations. On the other hand, they know that those challenges will be, by definition, difficult and risky. As a result, these managers are tempted to set the performance bar low. After all, difficult goals may generate grumbling in the ranks. And if subordinates fail to rise to the challenge, the managers will look bad.

Reducing expectations and making goals less challenging may solve these problems, but that is not what's best for the organization, or for you and your subordinates. The best course is to make goals achievable but challenging. Then, communicate frankly with your subordinates. Explain why these challenging goals were selected and why achieving them is so important, both for the organization and for your employees as individuals. Make sure that they see a personal benefit in goal achievement. Then, seek buy-in.

Be very clear about what successful achievement will look like, and how performance against those goals will be measured. Also,

depending on employee skills, consider whatever coaching or training will be needed to make the employee capable of meeting his or
her goals.

Get It on Paper

Once you and an employee have reached agreement on goals, document your conclusions in a formal memo that includes the
following:

- The date of your meeting

- Key points brought up by both parties

- The goals the employee has agreed to pursue

- What he or she will do to achieve them

- A description of any coaching or training you have agreed to
  provide

- The date on which the employee's performance will be formally appraised

Give a copy of that memo to the employee, and save one for yourself.

Documentation of this sort may seem unnecessary if your direct
reports are fairly senior. Their goals are broad and less easy to specify, and their freedom of personal action is substantial. However, this
documentation is recommended when direct reports are junior or
inexperienced or otherwise require close supervision.

Four Steps to Accomplishing Goals

Creating a clear set of goals is essential, but that is obviously not the
end of the road. Goals should be matched with practical plans for
achieving them. This is something that you and your subordinates
or team must do together. Converting goals into realities involves
four steps:

1. Break each goal down into specific tasks—with clear outcomes.

2. Plan the execution of those tasks—with timetables.

3. Gather the resources needed to fulfill each task.

4. Execute the plan.

This approach may sound very "by the numbers," but it is effective, especially with employees who need direction and close supervision. It is a very positive way for you and them to work together. Now, let's look in detail at these four steps.

Step 1. At the outset, determine which tasks are needed to accomplish your goals. Some of these tasks may have to be completed sequentially—for example, task A must be completed before you can begin task B. If this is the case, put the tasks in the right order. It's likely that other tasks can be completed simultaneously—you can assign some people to task A while another team attacks task B. If a task appears overwhelming, break it into smaller parts.

Step 2. Plan out each task, and give each a start and finish date. You might want to use a Gantt chart or some other time-scaled task diagram to make this clear to all. Gantt charts are the basic bar chart familiar to most people. These graphics are easy to read and clearly communicate what needs to be done in a particular time frame (figure 1-2). Set up milestones along the way, for example, "We should have the first stage of task A completed by 15 May of this year." Milestones break up long tasks into shorter, more manageable chunks, giving people greater assurance that the job can get done.

Step 3. As you schedule, remember that many efforts fail when planners overlook a significant part of the work or underestimate the time and resources required to complete it. So, once you've planned how each task will be executed, check your resources. Does the employee have sufficient time

FIGURE 1-2

Gantt chart example

Product development project

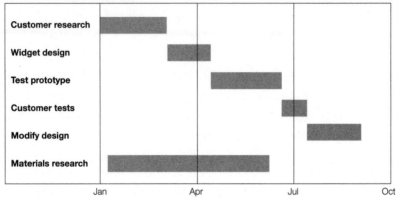

Source: *Manager's Toolkit: The 13 Skills Managers Need to Succeed,* Harvard Business Essentials series (Boston: Harvard Business School Press, 2004).

and equipment? Watch out for overloading. Do people have the training and know-how to get the job done?

Step 4. The execution of the plan is the final and most critical step. An experienced salesperson once described his secret for success this way: "First, plan your day—then work your plan." Working your plan means doing all the things you planned to do. This is where talk and good intentions must be transformed into real work.

Once you and your subordinates have agreed on goals, you need to have a meeting in which the four steps to those goals are made clear. Consider our earlier example of the sales manager and his field sales representative. The rep has been asked to increase sales in his territory by 10 percent, or $200,000. The goal itself says nothing about the tactics and the activities that must be brought to bear in squeezing out that increase. What should be the means toward that end? This is where one or more planning sessions between you and your employee can help. Let's listen in again:

Manager: A 10 percent increase won't be easy. You're bound to lose some business during the year from some accounts—that's natural. So you'll have to make up for those losses *and* develop new business in order to hit the $2.2 million target.

Sales rep: Yeah, I've been thinking about that.

Manager: And what ideas have you come up with? How do you plan to get from $2 million to $2.2 million?

Sales rep: Well, now that I have a good base of revenues in my existing accounts, I figure that I can do three things: improve after-sales service to existing accounts, prioritize my visits to sales prospects, and generate new sales in the Milwaukee area. I'm confident that good customer care will help me generate more sales from existing accounts. With the new products coming out in the spring, it's very likely that I will get more business from those companies. Prioritizing my field calls will help, too, because I'll be concentrating on the prospects that matter most.

Manager: That makes sense, but tell me your ideas for generating new business in the Milwaukee area.

Sales rep: As you know, Gizmo Products is opening a new production plant just outside Milwaukee. It's likely that Gizmo will include us as one of its suppliers, as it does at its other locations. I have to make sure that this happens.

Manager: That's just one new account. What else is in your sights?

Sales rep: Well, I know that two purchasing managers at Milwaukee area plants are retiring this coming summer. I've never had any success in dealing with either of them. They've given all the business to Acme and SmithCo. Once those guys are gone, new purchasing managers will be hired. And you know how new people are—they usually want to change things. That will create an opening for us. We have nowhere to go but up at those companies.

Manager: That sounds like a plan. Let's meet again next week and develop these ideas a bit more. In the meantime, give some thought to what you'll need from me in order to be successful—sales support, a bit more in your travel and entertainment budget, and so forth.

The sales manager and his subordinate have made a good start in moving from goal setting to activity planning. Further steps will flesh out those plans.

Summing Up

- Goals are the starting point for performance management.

- Create alignment between company, unit, and individual goals.

- Be sure that every subordinate has goals, understands them, and knows why they are important.

- Goals should be written down, put in a time frame, and supported by rewards.

- Be clear about how progress toward goals will be measured.

- Work with the employee in developing an action plan for achieving goals. That plan may include training and assistance from you.

Motivation

The Not-So-Secret Ingredient of High Performance

Key Topics Covered in This Chapter

- *Theories of motivation*

- *Intrinsic and extrinsic rewards*

- *The messy problem of incentive systems*

- *Ten motivational practices*

MOTIVATION IS THE next important piece of managing employee performance. It is, in fact, at the very heart of performance management— something that managers must attend to all the time. A person can understand goals and why they are important, but must also be motivated to pursue them. You can coach this same person to close performance gaps and improve productivity, but the employee won't take that coaching to heart if he or she is uninterested or unmotivated. You can spend hours on someone's annual performance appraisal and have a productive chat about it, but again, those hours will be wasted if the employee isn't motivated to improve.

This chapter explains some of the key theories of workplace motivation and the impact of rewards and incentives. It offers a number of things you can do to motivate the people who work for you.

Theories of Motivation

The principles of effective motivation have a long history. Although we tend to mark the beginning of that history with the Industrial Age, leaders and managers of every age undoubtedly understood the importance of motivation and probably experimented with different ways of inspiring it.

The classic theories of industrial management and organization were formulated in the late 1800s and early 1900s. These theories were less concerned with worker motivation than with the mechanisms of efficiency, predictability, and control. A business was conceptualized as a machine for producing goods and services, and people were simply among the parts of that machine. Frederick Taylor (1856–1915), credited as the father of scientific management, defined work in terms of coordinated, highly specified tasks designed for optimal efficiency, with little or nothing left to the judgment of production-line employees. This approach to work was supported by a particular view of human nature—or, should we say, the nature of industrial workers. In this view, employees were lazy and untrustworthy creatures. They could be motivated only by pay and the fear of dismissal and unemployment. Years later, Douglas McGregor would enshrine this view of human nature in what he called the Theory X approach to management.[1]

Managers who embrace Theory X have two motivational tools: the carrot and the stick—greed and fear. The Theory X work environment is characterized, as you'd imagine, by lots of prodding by the boss, tight control over employee work, and narrowly specified jobs.

The first chink in the armor of Theory X was exposed through experiments conducted during the 1920s by Elton Mayo at the Hawthorne Works, a Western Electric assembly plant in northern Illinois. Mayo hoped to determine the negative effects of fatigue, monotony, and unpleasant working conditions on job productivity and how these effects could be controlled or neutralized through improved lighting, more frequent rest breaks, different work hours, temperature, and other environmental factors. Using a control group of employees, he made frequent changes in their working conditions—pay, lighting levels, rest breaks, and so forth—always explaining his changes in advance. Productivity improved, but to Mayo's surprise, the improvements appeared to be independent of working conditions. He concluded that the workers performed better because management had demonstrated an interest in such improvements. Discussing changes in hours and breaks with workers had made them feel like members of a team, something they had not felt before.

Today, the *Hawthorne effect* refers to the productivity benefits that companies create when they pay attention to their employees and treat them as something other than mere cogs in the machinery of production. As interpreted by David Garvin and Norman Klein, Mayo's research showed that work output was not simply a function of a job's scientific design—as Taylor would have it—but also influenced by social norms, management-employee communications, and the level of employee involvement in workplace decisions: "Superior performance was linked to high levels of employee satisfaction; satisfaction, in turn, was tied to such non-economic factors as a sense of belonging and participation in decision making."[2]

Thanks to Mayo's groundbreaking work, we now understand that the workplace is a complex social system in which employee satisfaction and commitment affect performance. His findings stimulated new research and new thinking about what motivates people in the workplace. These, in turn, have done much to displace Theory X's dismal view of human nature. Theory X is not entirely false. People don't like to do certain painful things and are effort-averse. Incentives and job design can help improve performance, just as Theory X assumes. However, Theory X has generally given way to Theory Y (again formulated by Douglas McGregor), which postulates that people are not naturally slackers, but eager to work, to accept responsibility, and to produce good results. By implication, this view of human nature supports what we now think of as participative management, that is, a workplace system in which employees have greater discretion to think, act, and contribute to work plans. Indeed, one of the hard lessons that newly minted managers learn, according to studies by Harvard Business School's Linda Hill, is that the authority of their positions doesn't amount to much in terms of getting people to do things better or to do anything at all. These new managers discover that telling people what to do is far less motivating than actions that invite people to play bigger and more important roles. Managers can begin by explaining to subordinates *why* something must be done.[3]

What About Rewards?

The people who study motivators refer to two categories of rewards: intrinsic and extrinsic. *Intrinsic rewards* produce nonquantifiable personal satisfaction, such as a sense of accomplishment, personal control over one's work, and a feeling that one's work is appreciated. *Extrinsic rewards* are external, tangible forms of recognition such as pay hikes, promotions, bonuses, and sales prizes. Both types of rewards have a place in performance management, says Harvard Business School professor Brian Hall: "People are motivated by both intrinsic and extrinsic rewards."[4] Both intrinsic and extrinsic rewards motivate value-creating behavior and are effectively employed by managers. Most corporate reward systems, however, are built around extrinsic rewards, since money is the one tangible and highly manipulable incentive that corporations can give. A corporation cannot easily tell its sales reps, "Meet your sales goal this year, and we'll respect you more." But it can say, "If you make your quota, we'll pay you $5,000."

Intrinsic Rewards Generally Motivate Best

Some of the best advice on intrinsic and extrinsic rewards can be found in an old source: Frederick Herzberg's classic article "One More Time: How Do You Motivate Employees?" which was first published in 1968.[5] Herzberg found that extrinsic incentives such as bigger paychecks and plush offices don't necessarily make people work harder or better. When such motivators do succeed, the positive effects are short-lived. Recall the well-worn phrase "What have you done for me lately?" This explains why so few academics and practitioners categorize pay and perks as true motivators or commitment generators. Pay matters in the sense that a company has a difficult time recruiting and keeping good employees without a competitive level of pay and benefits. Money can be a huge motivator, but it often motivates the wrong behaviors—for example, encouraging people to cut ethical corners to earn a bonus or to game the reward system—and it does not build commitment. Consider Southwest Airlines. At the entry level, the carrier is one of the lowest-paying of the major airlines, yet it enjoys remarkable commitment from its people. Here, real motivators such as recognition and team spirit, when combined with adequate pay, have produced a committed workforce and the lowest level of employee turnover in the U.S. airline industry.

Herzberg's prescriptions remain valid today, and you can use them to enhance the motivation of all your subordinates. Figure 2-1 summarizes his findings. The term "hygiene factors" in the figure refers to the extrinsic elements of workplace life that affect job satisfaction. Note the importance of achievement and recognition on employee attitudes toward their jobs; note in comparison how little salary, status, and job security contribute to those attitudes.

These findings have been validated by more recent studies, including a 2000 survey of managers conducted by McKinsey & Company, in which 59 percent of respondents cited "interesting, challenging work" as critical in their decision to join or stay with a particular company. Financial rewards and career and advancement opportunities trailed at 39 percent and 37 percent, respectively. Just remember that a solid performance management system requires due respect to *both* intrinsic and extrinsic rewards.

Take a minute to think about the intrinsic and extrinsic rewards in your work environment. Are they sufficient? Are they effective? Do they motivate the right behaviors? Have you found the right balance between pecuniary and psychological rewards?

Unless you are a senior executive, your control of the extrinsic rewards offered by your company may be limited, but you do have substantial control over the intrinsic rewards experienced by your subordinates. At a minimum, do this:

- Compliment good work on the spot when you see it. "Thanks for doing that job so well." This will impart a highly motivating sense of personal accomplishment.

- Involve subordinates in planning. Their involvement will give them a feeling of control over their work—and people are more conscientious when they feel that they "own" their work. Perhaps the greatest reason that some people feel alienated from their work is that they lack control over how they spend their working days.

Simple actions like these can be highly motivating, and yet they cost nothing. You'll never go over your budget by doing these things.

FIGURE 2-1

Factors affecting the job attitudes, as reported in twelve investigations

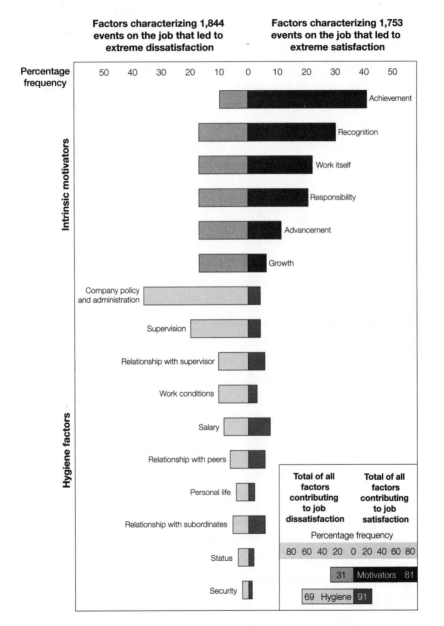

Source: Frederick Herzberg, "One More Time: How Do You Motivate Employees?" (HBR Classic), *Harvard Business Review,* January 2003. Used with permission.

The Challenge of Incentive Systems

A full discussion of incentive systems and the extrinsic rewards they offer is beyond the scope of this book. But to quote Brian Hall, the management of incentives is "generally difficult and messy":

> *Tensions arise over the division of pay as managers and workers routinely feel underpaid but rarely feel overpaid. The bonus plan, even when it is "working," never seems to drive precisely the right behavior. And subjective performance evaluations—especially those tied to rewards and punishments—are a dreaded task. They are fraught with anxiety, vulnerable to destructive politicization, and typically disliked by both those doing them and those receiving them.*[6]

Difficult and messy as they are, incentive systems are nevertheless essential since people are motivated by, among other things, many of the rewards that firms have to offer, and because workers in a competitive labor market demand them. So, if incentive systems are necessary, what should they look like? Conceptually, the answer to this question is simple: an incentive system should create alignment between desired performance and the rewards that employees value.

Achieving that alignment, however, is anything but simple. Indeed, perfect alignment is impossible. This is because the two elements that must be aligned—performance and "what people value"—are seldom clear and are often hard to measure. What, for example, do your subordinates value? Money, for sure. But how much money does it take to alter someone's behavior? Offer $100 to your sales reps if they hit their quotas, and you won't even get their attention. Offer $1 million, and you'll have their full attention, but that's not feasible. So, what is the right number? No one can say for certain. Worse, the right number for one person is the wrong one for someone else.

The performance element of alignment is equally uncertain. As described by Hall, measuring performance has three pitfalls:[7]

- **The uncontrollability problem.** Most performance measures, such as sales revenues and profits, are the result of factors that are both controllable (e.g., working harder and smarter) and uncontrollable (e.g., passage of adverse regulations). Almost all performance measures contain some level of uncontrollability.

- **The alignment problem.** Today's jobs typically require many tasks; some tasks are easy to measure (e.g., percentage of on-time deliveries), but others are not (e.g., courteous treatment of customers).

- **The interdependency problem.** Most outcomes are the result of work by many people, sometimes working together and other times working independently. Isolating the contribution of individual employees within these outcomes is nearly impossible.

These three problems are sources of inescapable conflict whenever companies design and implement incentive strategies. People complain that some incentives are unfair, reward some things but not others, fail to account for important efforts, are inequitable, and so forth. The subjective nature of performance evaluation is also a problem that defies precision and fairness—particularly for managers. Managers are supposed to develop the skills and careers of their people. But precise measurement of this duty is impossible. Managers are also required to coordinate their units' activities with those of others. How is this coordination to be measured?

Undeniably, these issues are difficult and messy. It's nearly impossible to satisfy everyone's sense of fairness. And some of the most important things that people must do are difficult to measure. But, as a manager, you cannot allow these impediments to keep you and your colleagues from working toward an effective incentive system.

Practical Tips for Motivating

Assuming that pay is fair and competitive, the things that make employees' jobs more interesting are the surest approach to individual motivation. How can you accomplish that? Here are some tried-and-true suggestions.

Demonstrate Trust

Some managers don't trust people to do a good job, and not surprisingly, these managers get what they expect. Others demonstrate greater faith in the inherent capability of their subordinates. These leaders trust each employee to do his or her job well, and—assuming that they have capable people on the payroll—such managers also generally get what they expect.

There are many ways to demonstrate trust: by removing some controls, or by asking a person to create a plan or schedule, or by putting a subordinate in charge of something you would normally handle. Demonstrate trust, and you will often be pleasantly surprised by the result. Just one caveat: be sure that the person to whom you extend trust understands that he or she is accountable for results, and provide oversight and support as needed.

Make Jobs More Complete

Theory X jobs are narrowly construed and highly specified. "Put bolt A into hole B." "Examine this loan application and check credit references; then, pass it on to John." This makes sense when people are viewed as extensions of a mechanized process and when they cannot be trusted to think, make judgments, or take independent action. But it is highly *de*motivating. People who have these types of jobs spend half the day grumbling and watching the clock. If you want to motivate people who seem ready for a new challenge, give them a more complete unit of work.

Team-based approaches to automobile assembly, research, new-product planning, and so forth, are examples of more complete jobs. These teams are given collective responsibility for planning their work, scheduling vacations, dealing with other units in the organization, and accomplishing other tasks. The same broad responsibilities can be designed into many jobs.

Psychologists Timothy Butler and James Waldroop have used the term "job sculpting" to describe their own form of job design.[8] Their prescription is to design jobs that match the "deeply imbedded life interests" of employees. For instance, a competent engineer with a deeply embedded life interest in counseling and mentoring might be asked to plan and manage the orientation of newly hired engineers. A salesperson with an interest in quantitative analysis might be given new duties working with the firm's market research analysts. Effective job sculpting is only possible, however, when a manager asks questions and listens carefully to what employees have to say about their real interests.

Introduce Challenge

People are often capable of handling tasks that are more complex and more demanding than their managers expect and that their job descriptions require. When presented with tougher assignments, employees will usually rise to the challenge. This is true in the workplace and in other aspects of daily life. Consider this true story:

> Every summer, the minister of a small Protestant congregation took a two-month vacation, and church trustees hired a divinity student to conduct Sunday services in his absence. This arrangement worked well. One year, however, they could not find a summer substitute and consequently asked church members to do the job.
>
> Joan, a social worker by profession, volunteered to lead one Sunday service that summer, even though she had absolutely no experience in this area. But Joan rose to the occasion. She recruited a pianist to provide special music, selected hymns for the congregation to sing, and asked others to read from Scripture. She even wrote and delivered the sermon.
>
> The people who attended Joan's service marveled at how well organized and polished it had been and at the thoughtfulness of her sermon. "If the minister ever quits," said one, "we should hire Joan."
>
> No one was more moved by Joan's performance as stand-in minister than Joan herself. Though the prospect of conducting a service had seemed daunting at first, she was pleased with how she had handled it. The entire experience was highly motivating, so motivating that Joan eventually quit her job and entered divinity school with the goal of becoming an ordained minister.

Joan's story exemplifies what people can accomplish when challenged and the motivational power of such experiences. By giving them opportunities to reach for higher levels of performance, you can provide similar motivation for the people who work for you.

Before you move on, take just a moment to think about the people who report to you. What new and challenging experiences would motivate them and—simultaneously—benefit the company?

Encourage Some People to Become Experts

Another way to motivate is to encourage certain individuals to become experts in subjects that interest them *and* that provide real value to the organization. Every operating unit requires resident experts: in quality control, information technology, process improvement, inventory control, budget matters, and dozens of other subjects. This expertise needn't be a full-time job to add real value to the unit. Simply having available people with deep knowledge in key areas can be a big plus. And giving a person leave to develop expertise can be highly motivating, instilling that person with greater pride and a sense of accomplishment and recognition at work. "Thanks for that article on process benchmarking. That's a technique we could use here. Would you be interesting in becoming our resident expert on benchmarking? Once you've mastered it, you could teach it to the rest of us."

Drive Out Fear

The late W. Edwards Deming (1900–1993) was one of the founders of the quality movement. His teachings on statistical quality control, and his fourteen principles of management, profoundly influenced business leaders, first in Japan and then in America. One principle he emphasized was "Drive out fear."

Fear of failure is sometimes useful. It reminds us that everything we do has consequences. But pervasive workplace fear demotivates people and discourages the behaviors that all businesses need in order to learn and succeed.

A fearful environment is created when bosses threaten or bully people or punish or fire them for making honest mistakes. Fear encourages excessive caution and motivates people to place self-protection ahead of the workplace activities that contribute to business success: collaboration, creativity, prudent risk-taking, and finding ways to improve work processes by admitting and learning from mistakes. As Harvard University professor Amy Edmondson has explained, organizations benefit when there is a climate of "psychological safety," which makes it possible for employees to shift their focus away from self-protection to more useful behaviors, such as discussing mistakes and sharing different perspectives. As she describes it, psychological safety does *not* imply a lack of consequences for poor performance; accountability must remain.[9]

Is fear lurking somewhere in your unit? If it is, find it and replace it with employee confidence. Doing so will have a positive impact on people's motivation.

Preserve Your Subordinates' Dignity

Be sure to maintain your subordinates' dignity and self-respect at all costs, even when you must be critical of their performance. You cannot motivate people whom you have stripped of dignity; some bosses do not understand this point and inadvertently behave in ways that humiliate their charges.

Have you ever witnessed a boss criticizing a subordinate in front of the person's peers? Incidents like this happen, and they violate one of the first laws of supervision: praise in public, criticize in private. The effect on the subordinate's dignity and motivation is usually devastating. Consider this true story:

Members of a district sales group were dining with their boss, the sales manager. They had just finished a long and tiring day of meetings. Disappointing sales over the past six months had added an element of tension to their gathering. As they lingered over too many after-dinner drinks, the manager threw out a question: "We have some great products. Why aren't they selling as well as they should?"

It was a complex question, and no one wanted to respond with a simple answer. Besides, the veterans in the group knew how argumentative and combative the boss could be after he'd had a drink or two. Frustrated by their silence, the boss restated the question and directed it to Dave, a young fellow who had joined the company just a year earlier.

Being inexperienced, Dave responded with what everyone at the table knew to be true, but which no one dared to acknowledge: "Well, lots of the buyers in my territory tell me that our returns policy is a problem for them."

True to form, the boss went ballistic and gave Dave a dressing-down in front of the entire group. "I'm sick and tired of these lame excuses from losers like you as to why you can't meet your sales goals," the boss ranted. His outburst continued for several minutes, with all of it directed at poor Dave.

Dave, in this case, had failed to meet his sales goals. But he was young and inexperienced and would probably have improved with time and proper coaching. But Dave was so humiliated by this incident that he soon left the company and joined a direct competitor and, before long, became a much more effective salesperson.

Sack the Slackers

Slackers are people who have no interest in doing more than what is minimally required. Their favorite expressions include "That's not my job" and "I'm not getting paid for that." Slackers put a damper on the enthusiasm and creativity that every company and every team needs to improve performance.

A timid manager will lower performance expectations to a level that accommodates the slow pace and low standards of slackers. Doing so is a huge mistake because it lowers the performance of the group as a whole and demotivates the best people. Instead of lowering standards, a manager should set them at a high but achievable level and challenge people to meet them. If slackers cannot or will not rise to the challenge, the manager has three options:

- Reclaim them through coaching

- Move them into positions more suitable to their level of work

- Dismiss them

Once slackers are reformed or removed, you'll find that motivating people will be less of an effort.

Empower, Don't Micromanage

People are generally more motivated when they feel as though they own what they do. Ask any entrepreneur. Ownership can mean legal ownership; it can also mean having control over the information and the decisions that involve one's immediate work. In either case, ownership means giving employees some responsibility for shaping their jobs, and even some voice in the design of the larger business structure.

In the world of Frederick Taylor, workers had no sense of ownership. They were merely cogs in the machinery of production and expected to follow orders. It's no wonder their bosses thought them dull, lazy, and uninterested in the goals of the enterprise.

If you want employees to feel and act like owners, start by looking at your company rule book. That's what Gordon Bethune did shortly after he took over failing Continental Airlines in 1994. One of the first things he did was burn the rule book—literally!

> *We had rules—specific rules—for everything from what color pencil had to be used on boarding passes to what kind of meals [the] delayed passengers were suppose to be given to what kind of fold ought to be put in a sick-day form. Even worse [our rule book] spelled out job responsibilities to such a fine degree that employees were utterly bound by arcane rules and demands, and the penalties for disobeying the rules were severe.*

Well, nobody likes to work like that. Nobody likes to be treated like a robot, like a little kid who can't solve a problem and make a contribution.

Very soon . . . we took a bunch of employees and a bunch of those manuals out to the parking lot and had the employees set fire to the manuals. I have to tell you, they didn't mind doing it. And we sent word into the field that henceforth we wanted our employees to use their judgment, not follow some rigid manual. When faced with an atypical situation, employees were instructed to do what was right for the customer and right for the company.[10]

Burning the rule book was quite a gesture! Bethune put a lot of decision-making power into the hands of frontline personnel along with the assurance that if they thought things through and didn't do anything "out of bounds," they would not be called on the carpet by management. And it worked. Morale at Continental took a huge step forward, as did productivity and profitability.

Hire Self-Motivated People

Perhaps the surest approach to staff motivation is to recruit people who are self-motivated. Some readers may say that this course of action has more to do with talent management than with performance management—and that would be true—but anything you can do to increase the level of motivation in your unit is fair game.

You can identify self-motivation in the hiring interview. Self-motivated people are generally optimistic, confident, goal-oriented, and ambitious. They have a can-do attitude. These people require little care and feeding; just point them in the right direction, support them with appropriate resources, and give them periodic praise and rewards, and they will get the job done.

Like slackers, the attitude of self-motivated people can be infectious. But unlike slackers, they infect their coworkers with an attitude that is positive and desirable. Just take care that management doesn't smother these self-motivated employees under a mountain of rules, give them too short a leash, or make them kowtow. Even the most self-motivated people can be dispirited by bad management— which suggests our final point.

Be a Good Boss

Motivation is often self-generating when people have a boss whom they respect and with whom they have a good relationship. A company can have terrific pay and benefits, employee-friendly policies, and all the other features that make for a healthy workplace, but a bad manager can neutralize these features and demotivate subordinates. Gallup researchers Marcus Buckingham and Curt Coffman put it this way:

> *Managers trump companies. It's not that . . . employee-focused initiatives are unimportant. It's just that your immediate manager is more important. She defines and pervades your work environment . . . [I]f your relationship with your manager is fractured, then no amount of in-chair massaging or company-sponsored dog walking will persuade you to stay and perform. It is better to work for a great manager in an old-fashioned company than for a terrible manager in a company offering an enlightened, company-focused culture.*[11]

So, what do we mean by being a good boss? As a general statement, a good boss not only achieves unit goals, but also earns the respect and trust of his or her subordinates by following these effective practices:

- Maintaining high standards for himself or herself and for subordinates

- Empowering people to do their jobs and advance their careers

- Acknowledging the contributions of others

- Providing objective feedback

- Rewarding genuine performance

- Taking an interest in the personal goals of subordinates

You surely know the difference between a good boss and a bad one, and you know how demotivating a bad one can be. So, if you want to motivate your people, be the best manager you can be.

Summing Up

- The Theory X view of human nature sees employees as lazy and untrustworthy—motivated solely by pay (the carrot) and fear of dismissal (the stick).

- The Theory Y view of human nature postulates that people are not naturally slackers, but are eager to work, to accept responsibility, and to produce good results.

- Pioneering research by Elton Mayo indicated that work output was influenced by social norms, management-employee communications, and the level of employee involvement in workplace decisions.

- Intrinsic rewards are those that produce nonquantifiable, personal satisfaction, such as a sense of accomplishment, personal control over one's work, and a feeling that one's work is appreciated. Extrinsic rewards are external, tangible forms of recognition such as pay hikes, promotions, bonuses, and sales prizes. Both types of rewards have a place in performance management.

- An incentive system should create alignment between desired performance and the rewards that employees value. Achieving that alignment, however, is difficult, and perfect alignment is impossible.

- Practical suggestions for motivating personnel—things that managers can do—include making pay fair and competitive; demonstrating trust; making jobs more complete; introducing challenge; encouraging some people to become experts; eliminating fear from the workplace; preserving the dignity of subordinates; sacking slackers; empowering people and avoiding micromanagement; hiring self-motivated people; and understanding the importance of being a good boss.

Monitoring Performance

Looking for What's Going Wrong and Right

Key Points Covered in This Chapter

- *A multistep process for understanding performance relative to goals*

- *The why and how of active listening*

- *Common causes of poor performance*

ONCE YOU AND your subordinates have agreed on goals and planned how to reach them, your employees should be ready to head off on the right trajectory. Anything you can do to motivate them will be a big plus.

At some point in the future, you and these employees will sit down together to appraise how well they have performed with respect to their goals. And you'll talk about new goals. That is the natural end of the performance management cycle—and the beginning of a new one. As a manager, however, you have many opportunities to provide positive interventions between these beginning and ending points. In fact, periodic progress checks are essential, for three reasons: first, they provide opportunities to remind employees about goals and the importance of these goals; second, periodic checks give you a chance to offer positive feedback about the good things that employees do. Finally, these checks can help you spot small problems before they become large ones. We call these problems, whether large or small, *performance gaps*; they are the difference between a subordinate's current performance and what is required. Here's an example:

> *Scott, a securities analyst employed by a regional brokerage firm, is generally effective in his role. However, the stockbrokers who rely on his reports have noted a gap between his performance and job requirements. Specifically, Scott's written reports are poorly organized and often fail to state clear conclusions. "What's the bottom line here?" complained one broker. "I cannot tell if you're recommending this stock or not."*

A manager's job is to identify performance gaps like this one and work with the employee to eliminate them.

People are not electric clocks. You cannot just set them and forget them. Instead, you need to observe performance quality and provide feedback on what appears to be going well and what is going poorly. This is particularly important in a fast-changing work environment. If a person is going off track, you must know about it early, before that employee wanders so far off target that personal goals become unattainable. Catch a problem early, and you and the employee will be in a better position to take corrective action and get back on track. This chapter will teach you how to work with employees to monitor performance and identify performance gaps while the disparities are still small and to find the root causes.

Observe and Gather Data

The first step in monitoring performance and detecting gaps is to understand the situation, the person, and the work being done. Direct observation is the best way to do this. Your mission should be to identify strengths and weaknesses and to understand the impact that the person's work and behavior has on coworkers and on the employee's ability to achieve specific goals.

There are many ways to gain a clear understanding of the situation, and we outline six of them here. First, you need to routinely check employee performance against stated performance metrics. If you've built monthly or quarterly milestones into each subordinate's annual goals, you will be able to spot good performance and performance gaps as they develop. Consider this example:

> *Nancy is worried about the performance of her subordinate, Eileen. Eileen's goal is to increase sales in her territory by 10 percent this calendar year. But the first-quarter results are now tabulated, and Eileen's sales are only 2 percent above last year's sales for the same period. She won't meet her annual goal if this trend continues.*

In this example, Eileen may or may not be having a problem. A huge order—one that will put her back on track—might be in the mail this very moment. Still, the first-quarter results are cause for concern, and Eileen's manager would be wise to talk with her. Questions like "What's going well?" "Are you having any problems?" and "Do you need help?" are useful.

Second, it is important to scrutinize the tasks that the employee is not doing well. What seem to be the causes? Also, look for behaviors that interfere with goal accomplishment, as in these examples:

Ralph observed something about Harriet, his subordinate, during a team meeting. She interrupted others frequently, preventing them from expressing their views. This was a negative for the team and for the teamwork on which Ralph's unit depended for its success.

Philip's sales report to his manager, Rita, was sketchy. "This report should give me a good idea of where we stand on key accounts," his boss told herself, "but Phil's report doesn't do that. It is vague and incomplete."

Third, avoid premature judgments. One or two observations may give an incomplete impression. So, continue observing, particularly if you have any doubts about your perceptions. For example, Harriet's manager should observe her behavior during several meetings and in other settings before concluding that she has a habit of interrupting others. Rita should do the same by asking Philip to submit reports on subsequent sales calls.

Fourth, try to draw facts from other sources when possible. When appropriate, discuss the situation in confidence with trusted peers or colleagues. Add their observations to your own. For example, Harriet's manager might ask this of a colleague: "My research assistant, Harriet, will be attending one of your meetings next week. I'd appreciate it if you would give me your assessment of her participation."

Fifth, if you notice poor performance, try to differentiate between a lack of skill and a lack of motivation. In her study of new managers, Harvard University professor Linda Hill found that most novice managers had trouble differentiating between these two sources of poor performance. Yet that differentiation is absolutely necessary in effecting a cure.

And finally, listen carefully. A person may be asking for your help, but you may not be hearing. Ask yourself, Have I passed up chances to listen? People don't always know what kind of help they need or exactly how to ask for it. Philip, the salesman, for example, might have dropped unheeded hints that he wasn't sure what information the boss was looking for in sales reports. So, when you see an opportunity, take the time to listen actively to your direct reports. What you hear will help you coach the person back to good performance.

Common Causes of Poor Performance

As you observe, keep in mind that poor performance may have a nonobvious cause that has nothing to do with lack of skill or motivation. And that cause may be something you can do something about. Here are a few possible reasons that people perform unsatisfactorily:

- **Bad processes.** This is the place to start. W. Edwards Deming, one of the great management teachers of the past century, warned business leaders that the source of unsatisfactory performance was usually bad work processes. Yelling at workers, bribing them with bonuses, and threatening them, he cautioned, will not produce better results if the work process is inherently flawed. If you want better performance, look to the work process before you look for faults in the people who run them.

- **Personal problems.** Something of a nonwork nature may be the root cause of poor performance: alcoholism, drug dependency, or conflict in the household. In many instances, the subordinate may be experiencing a work-life balance problem—that is, the demands of meeting the obligation to the company and to the individual's family may be unmanageable. You may be able to mitigate these problems if you can learn what they are. For example, if the person is having family problems because of too many evenings spent away from home on business trips, you can do something about that.

- **Relationship conflicts at work.** Anytime you throw people together in a workplace, there is a chance for conflict. Jealousy, a
  thwarted romantic interest, competition for attention or for a
  promotion, or simply a visceral dislike may produce conflict
  that impairs performance. If you can get to the bottom of the
  conflict, you may be able to neutralize it.

- **Work overload.** Even the most committed employee will burn
  out if you demand too much at too fast a pace. So, take a good
  look at how you are allocating the workload. You and the employees may have set the bar unreasonably high. (For more on
  burnout, see chapter 8.)

Are You Part of the Problem?

As you seek the cause of a performance gap, don't forget to look in
the mirror. It's possible that you are contributing to the problem.
John Gabarro and Linda Hill of Harvard Business School suggest
that you ask yourself these questions:[1]

- **How often and to what extent have I intervened in my subordinates' area of responsibility?** If their performance doesn't measure up, perhaps it is because you overruled their decisions or
  insisted that they follow *your* approach to completing the work.

- **To what extent have my own actions been a source of my subordinates' problems?** In one case, you might have taken away
  needed resources. In another, you might have given an assignment that was impossible to complete on time.

Move from Observation to Discussion

Once you've identified a performance problem, talk with the employee. But stick to observed actions and behaviors—leave supposi-
tions about the person's motivations out of it. For example, Philip's
boss could begin by saying something like this:

Phil, your last three sales reports have glossed over some important in-
formation. They didn't tell me what I needed to know about the status
of our most important accounts—that's information I must have.

Then, cite the impact of the person's performance problem or problematic behavior on individual or group goals and on coworkers. For
example, Philip's boss might say this:

When the national sales director calls me and asks for the status of our
key accounts, I can't say "I'm not sure." I need key information on
those accounts at my fingertips. And I depend on you and everyone else
in our sales district to get it for me.

When describing performance gaps and their impact, be truthful
and frank. People benefit from frankness, even though they don't like
getting negative news. Be frank, but soften the blow by leaving motives
out of the discussion. Otherwise, the person is likely to feel that he or
she is under personal attack. And when people feel they are being personally attacked, they become defensive and unreceptive to what you
have to say. Your assessment of motives would probably be pure specu-
lation, in any case. Here's an example of an assumed motive:

Phil, your failure to provide critical information in your reports tells
me that you're either hiding bad news or that you don't like this type
of work.

Be an Active Listener

To learn as much as possible from your discussion, practice active listening. Active listening encourages communication and puts other
people at ease. An active listener pays close attention to the speaker
and practices these other good listening skills:

- Maintain eye contact.

- Smile at appropriate moments.

- Be sensitive to body language.

- Listen first, and evaluate later.

- Never interrupt except to ask for clarification.

- Indicate that you're listening by repeating what was said about critical points, such as, "So if I hear you right, you're having trouble with . . ."

Active listening is one of the best tools for getting people to talk—and you want them to do most of the talking if your goal is to understand what is going wrong. You'll learn practically nothing when you're talking.

Ask the Right Questions

Asking the right questions will help you understand the other person and get to the bottom of performance problems. Questions take one of two forms: open-ended and closed. Each yields a different response. *Open-ended questions* invite participation and idea sharing. Use them to get the other person talking and for these purposes:

- To explore alternatives: "What would happen if? . . ."

- To uncover attitudes or needs: "How do you feel about our progress to date?"

- To establish priorities and allow elaboration: "What do you think the major issues are with this project?"

Closed questions, in contrast, lead to yes or no answers. Ask closed questions for these purposes:

- To focus the response: "Is the project on schedule?"

- To confirm what the other person has said: "So, your big problem is scheduling your time?"

When you want to find out more about the other person's motivations and feelings, use open-ended questions. This line of questioning can help you uncover the other person's views and deeper thoughts on the problem. This, in turn, will help you formulate better advice.

Form and Test Your Hypothesis

Observation, discussion, and questioning will eventually lead you to some hypothesis about the nature and cause of the performance gap. But your hypothesis may not be valid if your perspective is flawed or limited. To test your hypothesis, ask others what they think. They may have an entirely different viewpoint. For example, Harriet's habit of interrupting others may be viewed by her manager as stifling valuable dialogue; someone else, however, may applaud her strenuous articulation of her views. So, when appropriate, discuss these situations with trusted colleagues—in confidence, of course. Add their observations to your own.

> *As a final check, Harriet's manager, Ralph, asked another manager, Lena, for a favor. "Lena," he began, "I notice that you'll be attending my group's planning meeting this afternoon." She nodded in agreement. "Would you do something for me?" He went on to ask Lena to observe Harriet's participation in that meeting and let him know her impression. He was careful not to say, "Tell me if she seems to interrupt others." Doing so might have influenced Lena's thinking.*
>
> *Ralph saw Lena in the coffee room the next day. When no one else was in earshot, he asked for her impression of Harriet's participation in the previous day's meeting. "She's smart and very knowledgeable," Lena said. "But she's not a good listener." Ralph asked what made her say that. "Well," Lena continued, "she interrupts other people when she should be listening to what they have to say."*

Feedback from other sources provides a useful reality check of your own views, which may be prejudiced or inaccurate. It may also prevent you from making a big issue of a small performance problem.

The process we've described—observation, questioning, and forming and testing a hypothesis—will eventually help you identify the cause of the performance problem. The cause may be a *skill deficiency,* poor time management or personal work habits, lack of motivation, conflict with another employee, or poor direction on your part. Whatever the cause, having identified it, you are now in a position to do something about the performance gap. In many instances, doing something involves coaching, the subject of our next chapter.

Summing Up

- Monitoring performance and detecting gaps can be accomplished by a process that involves direct observation, data gathering, discussion, active listening, thoughtful questioning, and forming and testing a hypothesis.

- As you seek the cause of a performance problem, begin with the work process itself. No amount of motivation, coaching, or cajoling can overcome flaws caused by a bad work process.

- Look in the mirror. Determine how much good or bad performance is directly related to your management role.

Closing Gaps and Improving Performance

The Basics of Coaching

Key Topics Covered in This Chapter

- *Coaching as a four-step process*

- *Why agreement on coaching goals is essential*

- *Action plans for coaching*

- *Giving and receiving feedback*

COACHING IS AN interactive process through which managers and supervisors aim to close performance gaps, teach skills, impart knowledge, and inculcate values and desirable work behaviors. It is a powerful method for strengthening the organization's store of human capital. Good managers are always looking for coaching opportunities.

Coaching can rekindle motivation and help your subordinates with numerous important aspects of effective performance:

- Closing performance gaps

- Overcoming personal obstacles

- Achieving new skills and competencies

- Preparing themselves for new responsibilities

- Becoming more motivated

- Managing themselves more effectively

Good coaching produces better performance, greater job satisfaction, and higher motivation. It may also improve your working relationship with subordinates, making your job as manager much easier. Formal skill training is another approach to closing performance gaps and upgrading the capabilities of your employees. But that's another subject, which we'll address later in the book. This chapter explains how to identify coaching opportunities, then gives you a four-step process for doing it well.

Coaching Opportunities

Chapter 3 explained how to identify performance gaps. Effective coaching can often close these gaps. But coaching isn't simply a tool for curing performance problems; it's also a practical approach for providing subordinates with new skills—skills they need if they are to take on responsibilities that are more demanding. Consider this example:

> *You know from working with Claudia that she has real managerial potential. She is a fast learner, works well with other people, and is committed to the company's goals. You'd like to advance her to a higher level, and she has expressed an interest in moving up, but she isn't quite ready. One thing is holding her back: her reluctance to confront difficult and argumentative people. That weakness is blocking her upward mobility. She might get through that roadblock if someone would give her some pointers and encouragement.*

Do you have subordinates like Claudia? What coaching opportunities do you see for them? Are you doing anything about them? Answer these questions by making a list of all the people whom you currently deal with and who would benefit from effective coaching, as in table 4-1. Then, prioritize the list to identify the greatest opportunities. Concentrate on these before you move on to others.

TABLE 4-1

Current coaching opportunities

Subordinate	Comment
Claudia	Has trouble with difficult people. She is too nonconfrontational.
Lynn	Must learn to delegate—thinks she must do everything herself.
Philip	Needs help with writing his sales reports. His reports are not well organized.
Carlos	Definitely needs meeting management skills. The one meeting I put him in charge of was a disaster.

Chances are that each of your direct reports could benefit from coaching in some way—either from you or from someone with unique skills. You probably have plenty to share with others. But you don't have all the time in the world for sharing it. So, target your coaching to situations that most demand it—where you will get the highest return on your commitment of time and effort. The most productive opportunities generally arise in these situations:

- A new subordinate needs direction.

- A direct report is almost ready for new responsibilities and just needs a bit more help.

- A problem performer could be brought up to an acceptable level of work if given some guidance.

- A newly minted manager under your wing is still behaving as through he or she were an individual contributor.

Do you have subordinates like these? If so, then you, the subordinates, and your organization could probably benefit from effective employee coaching.

Coaching is generally accomplished through a four-step process:

1. Observation, in which you identify a performance gap or an opportunity to improve

2. Discussion and agreement

3. Active coaching

4. Follow-up

Step 1, observation, is an activity you can do without directly engaging your subordinates and was covered in the previous chapter. The other steps require more direct interaction with your employees and will be addressed here.

Discussion and Agreement

When you've pinpointed a coaching opportunity, talk it over with your subordinate to assure that he or she agrees that there is (1) a problem that needs fixing or (2) an opportunity to move know-how or job performance up a notch or two. Agreement is the foundation of successful coaching. You build agreement as you pursue the coaching objectives. Do the two of you see the problem or opportunity the same way? Agreement is absolutely essential because you cannot successfully coach a person who sees no need for coaching or who has a different perspective on the problem. During the discussion step, you and your subordinate should talk about the purpose of your coaching: to improve delegating skills, to correct a problem in how monthly reports are being written, or whatever the issue happens to be. You should also brainstorm possible solutions and generate some excitement about the good things that will follow! (See "Coaching As Management" to learn about the pitfalls of not following this collaborative approach.)

Coaching As Management

People who've earned their stripes in command-and-control organizations are inclined to see managing and coaching as two very different activities:

Managing focuses on	Coaching focuses on
• Telling	• Exploring
• Directing	• Facilitating
• Authority	• Partnership
• Immediate needs	• Long-term improvement
• A specific outcome	• Many possible outcomes

The different foci of these activities explain why some command-and-control managers have so much trouble coaching their subordinates. But in organizations where employees have substantial powers to make decisions and act, and where teamwork is emphasized, coaching is a very real part of managing.

Active Coaching

Now that the two of you are ready to begin active coaching, revisit your earlier discussion and confirm your agreement on what the goals of your coaching should be. Since days or weeks may have passed since your initial discussion, make sure that you have a shared understanding. Make this the first order of business, as in the following example:

> Well, Lynn, I'm glad that we could schedule this next hour to talk about delegating and how you can become better at it. As a new manager, you're surely discovering what I discovered years ago when I was in your position: that there is never enough time in the day. The only way to get your work done is to delegate some of it effectively.
>
> But before we get started, let's refresh our memories about what we discussed last week. We agreed that it would be a good thing to meet for an hour or so every week to talk about delegating and to review your progress. You said that you would like to reach the point where you could confidently delegate three or four time-consuming tasks to your subordinates. Is that how you remember our discussion?

Notice in the example how Lynn's boss stated his understanding of the earlier discussion and asked for Lynn's affirmation. Notice, too, how he stated the benefit of achieving the goal: "The only way to get your work done is to delegate some of it." The person you are coaching must see a clear benefit in attaining the stated goal.

At this point, ask for a formal agreement on the goal: "So, are we agreed that our goal is to make you a better delegator?" You must get to a point of mutual agreement on the goal of coaching.

Create an Action Plan

Once you have reached an agreement, the next step is to develop an action plan that will produce the end you both desire. An *action plan* contains a statement of goals and the measures of success, a timetable, and a clear indication of how the coach and the coachee will work together. The benefit of a formal action plan is that both parties know exactly what is expected, their mutual obligations, and how success will be measured. This eliminates the possibility of either party's saying, "Oh, this wasn't what I had in mind" when the coaching program has ended.

Not every coaching situation requires an action plan. Many, in fact, can be handled spontaneously and on the spot, as in this example:

> *A subordinate handed his boss a report on the second-quarter 2005 sales results of each of the company's sales districts, arranged in column form. "Here's my first draft," he said, "I can have a finished version for you this afternoon. Any comments?"*
>
> *The boss glanced at the spreadsheet. "This looks good, but can I make a suggestion?"*
>
> *"Sure."*
>
> *"Your report will be more useful if you show second-quarter sales for each district in both 2005 and 2006. That way, readers could see how each district has fared year-to-year. Do you see what I mean? I learned that trick from my first boss back in the Late Bronze Age."*
>
> *"I see the point," he said. "For each region, I could add a column showing second-quarter sales from the previous year and the calculated percentage change."*
>
> *"Yes, try that in your next draft," said his boss. "Do you know where to find last year's sales figures by region?"*
>
> *The boss went on to discuss numeric reports like this one, how the company's decision makers used them, and how comparative data helps managers put business results in perspective.*

In this example, the boss didn't develop a coaching plan; instead she saw an opportunity to coach her subordinate on the spot. Notice how she complimented the employee on his draft before suggesting how it could be improved. That's on-the-spot coaching, and it is often the most effective coaching method.

Other situations, particularly those with larger scope, benefit from an action plan. One clear example is when a subordinate must bring performance up to a higher standard within a certain time or risk dismissal. Another is a situation in which you are trying to develop a subordinate's skills to meet the requirements of the job or of a promotion. Here, planning is very useful. For example, consider the case of Harris, a subordinate of Mark. Harris must be proficient in the use of the company's spreadsheet and presentation software before he can advance. In this case, the action plan would most likely include a variety of elements:

- **A statement of the current situation.** Harris currently has only a rudimentary understanding of DigitCalc, the corporation's adopted spreadsheet program, and has never used CompuPoint graphic presentation software. The ability to use these programs for market analysis and presentations to management is required for advancement to an associate market analyst position.

- **Specific goals.** At a minimum, proficiency will be evidenced by an ability to develop market segment data in spreadsheet form, convert that numerical data into bar charts and pie charts, and accurately communicate all data by means of CompuPoint presentations.

- **A timeline.** In their action plan, Mark and Harris would agree on certain milestones of progress, such as these:

  By March 15, Harris will demonstrate proficiency with DigitCalc via the first-quarter marketing report.

  By April 15, he will demonstrate proficiency with CompuPoint via a hypothetical market analysis presentation.

  By May 15, he will develop a sample presentation using both programs and actual market research data.

- **Action steps.** Harris will use tutorials recommended by the information technology (IT) department and will prepare a series of presentations using those programs and current market data.

- **The coach's role.** Mark will meet periodically with Harris to provide coaching and critiques as Harris works toward his objectives. Mark will also provide Harris with technical assistance from the IT department as needed.

Table 4-2 is a sample action plan you may want to adapt for your own purposes.

Should the coach be the author of the action plan? Not usually. The employee should be given the opportunity to develop a plan. Say something like this: "What would you propose as a solution?" Putting the ball in the employee's court will make the person more responsible for the solution and, hopefully, more committed to it. As the employee describes the plan, challenge the assumptions of the plan and offer ideas for making the plan stronger. If the employee cannot put a credible plan together, take a more active approach. In either case, seek agreement and commitment from the employee to every part of the plan.

Begin Coaching

As you begin coaching, communicate ideas so that the person receiving them can grasp and appreciate their value. For some people, you might communicate through simple telling: do this, then do

TABLE 4-2

Sample action plan

Goal: Learn to use DigitCalc and CompuPoint in market analysis reports and presentations

Timeline: By May 15

Milestone	Measure(s) of success	Review date
Become proficient in DigitCalc	Use DigitCalc on first-quarter marketing report	March 15
Become proficient in CompuPoint	Use CompuPoint to prepare hypothetical market analysis presentation	April 15
Demonstrate independent ability to use both software utilities in work-related projects	Develop presentation using real data and both DigitCalc and CompuPoint software	May 15

Source: Harvard ManageMentor® on Coaching, adapted with permission.

that. Some people learn best through examples. Still others learn best when they work hand-in-hand with someone else. For an example of this last method, let's return to the case of Harris, who needed to learn the use of the spreadsheet and graphic presentation software. His boss, Mark, could have tossed a pile of user manuals on Harris's desk and said, "Study these. They will teach you what you need to know." Instead, Mark set up a projector and screen and asked Harris to take a seat.

"I'm going to treat you to a slide show that Janice Bowman and I presented to senior management two years ago," he told Harris. "It's our business case for the QuikPik product line that was eventually launched last October. The presentation is based on market research data similar to the data you'll be working with if you advance to the associate market analyst level. I'll show you the same data in spreadsheet form after you've seen the presentation."

Mark presented the fifteen-slide QuikPik case, explaining as he moved forward. Some slides summarized customer research findings in short bullet points. Others represented numerical market data in clearly rendered charts: market-share data in pie charts and forecasted cash flows in bar-chart form. Harris could see how the slide presentation, when coupled with Mark's narrative, gave company executives the information they needed to make a decision.

"The reason I showed you this presentation," Mark said, "is to help you see the result of good market analysis—namely, data arrayed in ways that communicate insights to decision makers. If you want to be a market analyst, this is something you must learn how to do. As you learn how to use DigitCalc, you'll see how you can convert data into charts that help people grasp the data more easily."

After some discussion, Mark ended the coaching session. "Here's a tutorial for learning to use DigitCalc," he said as he handed over a CD-ROM. "It will teach you the basics. Over the next week, I'd like you to use spreadsheet data to create bar and pie charts like the ones I've just shown. That will be good practice. If you get stuck, talk to Janice, who has agreed to help. She's a DigitCalc whiz. When we meet again next week, we'll review your charts. I'll also have some new market data that we can develop into presentation slides."

Notice in this example how Mark communicated his ideas so that Harris could readily appreciate their value. Rather than expecting that Harris learn on his own through tutorials, Mark showed his subordinate a complete example of what Harris should aim to achieve for himself. Mark coached in a manner that made it easier for Harris to learn.

What tasks are you trying to help your subordinates perform? Have you provided them with tangible examples of good work or good practice? Have you communicated in ways they can appreciate and grasp? Your coaching will be most successful if you use a combination of telling and inquiry in your communications. Telling a person what to do and how to do it is usually necessary, and telling or showing people how to do things is also effective and saves time. But learning has a bigger impact when people figure things out for themselves. (See "Tip: Begin with the Easy Things" if you are not sure what to focus on when a subordinate is facing several challenges.)

Give and Receive Feedback

Giving and receiving feedback is an essential part of coaching—and management in general. This give-and-take of information should

Tip: Begin with the Easy Things

Some employees need coaching in several areas, which raises the question of where to begin. There's an old saying that we cannot learn to run until we've first learned to crawl and then to walk. Mastery is, in fact, accomplished through progressive steps. This is true whether you are learning the martial arts, piloting an airplane, or managing and controlling a large organization. So, begin with the easy things, and move progressively toward more difficult coaching tasks. This approach will reduce the risk of failure and prepare your coachee to attack more difficult problems with greater confidence.

go on throughout the active coaching phase as the coach and subordinate identify issues to work on, develop action plans together, work on problems, and assess results.

Some people fail to distinguish between praise and positive feedback, and between criticism and negative feedback. Let's make these distinctions clear before we move on. Praise is simply a pat on the back for good work: "You did a very good job with that prototype demonstration." Positive feedback goes further, identifying particular actions of merit: "I liked how you handled the prototype demonstration. The way you began with the underlying technical challenges, described how those challenges were addressed, and finished with the actual demonstration helped us all understand the technology."

Criticism and negative feedback follow this same pattern. Criticism is a kick in the pants and explains very little: "That demonstration was poor. People in the audience were either bored or confused." Negative feedback, in contrast, brings in the details, providing a basis for discussion and improvement: "I think your demonstration suffered from a lack of organization. The good thing was that you showed that the prototype worked. But as a viewer, I wasn't sure of the problem the prototype aimed to solve. Nor were the technical challenges made clear. Let's work on these."

Here are a few tips for giving feedback:[1]

- **Focus on improving performance.** Don't use feedback simply to criticize or to underscore poor performance. You should bring attention to work that is done poorly, but it is equally important to give affirming, reinforcing feedback on work that is done well—that helps people to learn from what they did right.

- **Keep the focus of feedback on the future.** Focus on issues that can be improved in the future. In other words, prioritize! For example, if a subordinate's misstep was a onetime event unlikely to be repeated, you might let it go.

- **Provide timely feedback.** Arrange to give feedback as soon as possible after you've observed a behavior you want to correct or reinforce. "This slide is excellent, Harris. Your bar chart conveys the data in a single glance." Wait only to gather all the necessary information.

- **Focus on behavior, not character, attitudes, or personality.** This practice will prevent the other person from feeling personally attacked. A person who feels under attack is not in a mood to learn.

- **Be specific.** Instead of saying, "You did a really good job during that meeting," offer something more concrete, such as "The graphics you chose for your presentation were very effective. You used just the right number of charts to convey the information without burying us in data."

Since coaching is a two-way activity, be as prepared to receive feedback as to give it. Without feedback from the other person, there is no communication. And without communication, you cannot know if your advice is clear and complete, or if your coaching is even helpful. So, encourage feedback from the coachee: "Is what I said clear?" "Is this where you are having the most trouble?" "Is this helping?"

When receiving feedback, give the other person your undivided attention. Provide evidence of your full attention by periodically paraphrasing what you understood the other person to say. "So, if I understand you correctly, you are not getting the staff support you need to get this job done correctly and on time. Is that right?"

Separate fact from opinion. For example, if someone says that your calculations are wrong and then points out the error, that is a fact. If he or she instead says, "Your suggestion is unworkable," that's an opinion. Opinions should not be discounted—either yours or the other person's—but they shouldn't carry the same weight as demonstrated facts. So, push back when feedback comes in the form of an opinion. Try to convert an opinion into specific information. For example, if the other person says that you have shown no interest in the coaching plan he or she developed, don't say, "You're wrong. I *am* interested." Instead say, "What did I say or do that made you think I wasn't interested in your plan?" The same holds true for positive feedback. If your subordinate tells you that your coaching suggestions were helpful, ask for specifics. "How were my suggestions helpful to you?" "Is there anything more that I can do to help you with this problem?" (See also "Tips on How to Get Feedback from Uncommunicative People.")

Finally, thank the person for the feedback, both positive and negative. Doing so will improve trust and be a model of productive behavior to the person you are coaching.

Tips on How to Get Feedback from Uncommunicative People

Some people are not very responsive, especially when they are being coached about a performance problem. Your attempts to solicit feedback may only elicit a perfunctory nod, as if to say, "Yes, I understand." But that isn't feedback, and it's no assurance that the person really understands.

How can you get feedback from uncommunicative people? Training consultant Nancy Brodsky of Interaction Associates, LLC, makes these suggestions:[a]

- Rehearse how you will respond if there is no reaction.

- Practice speaking slowly and taking long pauses.

- Make it clear that you expect a reply—and are willing to wait for one.

- Ask open-ended questions that help the person come up with a plan.

[a]Harvard ManageMentor® on Giving and Receiving Feedback, adapted with permission.

Adopt an Appropriate Approach

There are two basic coaching approaches, and you should adopt the one that best matches the situation.[2] In some cases, you must adopt a direct approach. *Direct coaching* involves showing or telling the other person what to do; it is most helpful when you are working with people who are inexperienced or whose performance requires immediate improvement. Other situations call for *supportive coaching*; here the coach acts more as a facilitator or guide (table 4–3).

Supportive coaching is especially important for individuals who meet current standards of performance but need to prepare to take

TABLE 4-3

Direct versus supportive coaching

Coaching style and purpose of action	Example
Direct	
Developing skills	Instructing a new employee who needs to develop skills in your area of expertise, or matching the employee with another coach who has the skills needed
Providing answers	Explaining the business strategy to a new employee
Instructing	Indicating the most expedient way to do a task, or working together with the employee on a task or project in which he or she can learn from you—e.g., a joint sales call
Supportive	
Facilitating problem solving	Helping others find their own solutions
Building self-confidence	Expressing confidence that an individual can find the solution
Encouraging others to learn on their own	Allowing individuals with new responsibilities to learn on the job, even if it means risking mistakes
Serving as a resource to others	Providing information or contacts to help others solve problems on their own

Source: Harvard ManageMentor® on Coaching, adapted with permission.

on new or greater responsibilities. With this group, be sure to employ these effective coaching techniques:

- Recognize the good work the employees are doing. Without making promises, indicate that opportunities for advancement are available.

- Invite them to use their experience and expertise to coach others.

- Enter into realistic discussions about career goals.

- Specify the knowledge, skills, and commitment required for different career moves.

- Ask these employees to describe the skills and knowledge they must develop if they are to move ahead.

- Develop a mutually acceptable plan for their acquiring the requisite skills and knowledge.

- Follow up on that plan at regular intervals with measurement and feedback.

Follow–up

Effective coaching includes follow-up that checks progress and understanding. This is the final step of the coaching process. Follow-up gives you an opportunity to prevent backsliding, reinforce learning, and continue individual improvement. Your follow-up might include asking what is going well and what is not. For example, Mark, the boss who was developing the presentation skills of Harris, followed up his initial coaching session one week later.

"Last week, I gave you that tutorial for learning to use DigitCalc, our spreadsheet and chart-making software. Have you made any progress?"

When Harris responded in the affirmative, Mark suggested that he and Harris use DigitCalc to create a set of pie and bar charts. "Here's a CD with a DigitCalc spreadsheet file. It has market data on one of our new products. Why don't you open this file and show me what you can do with the data—just as you would if you were preparing a presentation for our marketing group?"

Follow-up sessions like this one are opportunities to check progress, praise progress, and look for chances for continued coaching and feedback. If an action plan needs modification, the follow-up meeting is the place to do it. So, always follow up with these steps. Here are some of the things you can do:

- Set a date for a follow-up discussion.

- Check the progress that the individual has made.

- Continue to observe.

- Ask how the other person is doing and what you can do to help.

- Identify possible modifications to the action plan.

- Ask what worked and what could be improved in the coaching session.

If you're a new manager or new at coaching, your first efforts may feel uncomfortable and may not be entirely effective. Don't be discouraged. Don't stop. Instead, remember that you will get better with practice. So, watch for opportunities to coach the people under your supervision, prepare yourself, and then jump in.

Summing Up

- Coaching is an interactive process through which managers and supervisors aim to close performance gaps, teach skills, impart knowledge, and inculcate values and desirable work behaviors.

- Coaching is a four-step process: observation, discussion and agreement, active coaching, and follow-up.

- As you begin active coaching, confirm whatever agreement you and your subordinate had reached on the goals of your coaching. Before you jump in, make sure that you and the other person have a shared understanding of what you aim to achieve.

- Make sure that the other person sees a clear benefit in your mutual coaching goals. You won't accomplish much if your subordinate fails to see a benefit in the coaching exercise.

- Except for spontaneous, on-the-spot coaching, use a mutually agreeable action plan that will produce the end you both desire. An action plan defines goals and measures of success, creates a timetable, and gives a clear indication of how the coach and the coachee will work together.

- A combination of telling and inquiry is often effective in engaging the other person. Here, you tell someone how to do a task and then ask, "Do you foresee any problem with doing that yourself?"

- Allow for feedback from both parties—it's an essential part of the coaching process.

- Plan for follow-up on your coaching experience. Follow-up can prevent backsliding, reinforce learning, and continue individual improvement.

5

Becoming a Better Coach

Beyond the Basics

Key Topics Covered in This Chapter

- *Delegating coaching responsibilities*

- *Three conditions that improve coaching results*

- *Common mistakes made by coaches—and the remedies*

- *The challenge of team coaching*

KNOWING THE *why* and *what* of coaching is enough to get started, but is insufficient to make you excel as a coach. And becoming an excellent coach can truly enhance your career in management.

Like many interpersonal activities, good coaching is often the product of personal qualities and interpersonal skills, neither of which can be taught in any book, this one included. Nevertheless, you can learn some things that will improve your coaching experiences. One lesson is knowing when *not* to coach; some situations are better resolved through other means. Then, too, some coaching can be delegated, saving you lots of time and perhaps improving results. Delegating is one of a manager's most important tools, and coaching, like some other managerial chores, can sometimes be delegated to competent subordinates. This chapter will help you identify situations in which delegation makes sense.

You can also improve your coaching by creating a climate in which success is more likely. A hostile climate is obviously not conducive to the two-way participation required for effective coaching. In these pages, you'll learn of three conditions that support coaching effectiveness. The chapter ends with a number of dos and don'ts observed by every good coach.

Conserve Time and Energy

Coaching consumes every manager's most valuable and limited resource: time. All managers are pressed for time: for budgeting, planning, hiring and firing, meetings, and the countless other things that crowd their daily calendars. As a result, most managers underinvest in coaching. And when they do coach, being pressed for time, they either do the coaching themselves, figuring that this is the quickest way to deal with the problem, or they micromanage, telling their employees exactly what to do and how to do it—in other words, being "bossy." Both behaviors are demotivating to employees.

You must be very judicious in the amount of time you allocate to coaching. Coaching is important, but so are many other things.

Know When to Coach and When Not to Coach

You can make the most of your time by recognizing that some situations benefit more from coaching than do others. For example, Rolf had a problem writing reports; they were extremely wordy, lacked the headings and bullet points that make for faster reading, and never contained an executive summary. His boss, Karl, was eager to help Rolf for two very good reasons: first, Karl had to read those reports, and second, Rolf would not realize his career potential without improvement in that area. But Karl knew that Rolf wasn't even aware of the problem. Thus, coaching him might be a waste of time—time Karl could spend on something with a higher payoff potential. He decided that the best course of action was to make Rolf aware of the problem and give him an opportunity to take care of it on his own.

Delegate When Possible

As a manager, you have learned to delegate responsibility for many tasks, freeing up time you can allocate to issues that are more important. Delegation has another benefit: it gives the delegated people opportunities to take on more responsibility and develop their skills.

Some coaching situations may be candidates for delegation when someone else is able to do the job and perhaps do the job better than you. Consider Rolf's report-writing problems.

"Rolf," said Karl, "you did a very good job with those reliability tests. If you hadn't found those problems, we might have approved the current

design and sent it on to manufacturing. That would have been a costly mistake. So thanks for that."

After a brief conversation about Rolf's testing method and his findings, Karl brought up the report. "You managed to get all the important information into this report," he said, holding up the document. "But can I give you some friendly advice?"

"Sure, what is it?" Rolf asked.

"Make your reports more reader-friendly. Some of the people who read these things are simply looking for a summary—and they won't find it here—which means that they won't read anything you've written. Others are content to skim for key points and conclusions. And then there are a few techno-nerds, like me, who want all the details. Report writing that meets these different needs in a single document is an art. Unfortunately, it's not an art they taught either of us in engineering school."

"I know what you mean," Rolf responded. "I'm never sure how I should report my findings. As a result, it usually takes me more time to write the report than run the actual tests. And if people aren't reading them, what's the point?"

"Exactly," said Karl. "So, would you like some help on this?"

"Yes, I'd welcome it."

"Good," Karl affirmed. "For starters, I'll have you work with Sophia, a staff technical writer. Sophia isn't an engineer, but she speaks our language, and she has helped other people improve their writing. I've already talked to her about this and given her a copy of your report. By the time she's through with you, Rolf, you'll be a prime candidate for the Pulitzer Prize in the report-writing category."

"I can't wait," Rolf laughed. "By the way, what's the cash reward these days for a Pulitzer Prize?"

Notice how the boss in this situation began with a compliment, then gained his subordinate's interest in a plan of improvement. But in this case, the boss didn't suggest developing an action plan or a time when they might work together. Instead, he effectively delegated the coaching task to someone else—and to someone who had more to contribute than he.

How many opportunities do you have to delegate coaching to other qualified and willing parties? In some cases, your human resource department may be able to help with tutorial programs and contracted trainers. Remember also that you are giving the people to whom you delegate coaching tasks an opportunity to sharpen their skills—skills they will need as they advance in their careers. Thus, delegation has three benefits:

1. It conserves your time and energy.

2. It provides personal development for one of your subordinates—the designated coach.

3. It helps the coachee become more proficient.

As a final note, never forget this rule of effective delegation: the person delegated must assume responsibility for the outcome. Thus, if Sophia accepts the task of coaching Rolf, she must assume responsibility for Rolf's report-writing progress. Accept the chore, accept responsibility for the outcome. Otherwise, the outcome is likely to be disappointing.

Create the Right Climate

Another thing you can do to become a better coach is to pay attention to the psychosocial climate in which coaching takes place. The results of coaching generally improve when executives, managers, and supervisors create a climate conducive to learning. That climate is characterized by these intangible but important features:

- Mutual trust

- Accountability for results

- Motivation to learn and improve

Let's consider each of these characteristics in detail.

Mutual Trust

Have you ever helped a child learn to ride a bicycle? It is a scary experience for a child. The youngster is trying to balance an unfamiliar piece of equipment and make it move forward at the same time. An added fear is knowing that losing control or balance will send him or her crashing to the hard pavement. Reassurances such as "It's easy once you get the hang of it" or "I know this is scary; I had to do this myself when I was your age" may be helpful to the child. But what matters most is the voice of someone the child trusts saying, "Don't worry; I'll catch you if you begin to fall." The confidence that stems from that reassuring statement will divert the child's attention from fear to the skill he or she hopes to master.

Whether you are helping a child learn to ride a bicycle or helping a subordinate learn a winning approach to closing a sale, trust matters. Trust has several sources:

- Demonstrated concern for the other person's well-being and success. People trust those who have their best interests in mind. A good manager earns that trust by showing empathy for subordinates. When asking someone to work late on a project, the good boss will also ask, "Would this upset any plans you've made with your family or friends?" Alternatively, he or she may say, "I know that this is an imposition—you have other things to do after five o'clock." Trust is also established when a boss demonstrates a genuine interest in a subordinate's career success. "I really trust my boss," Sheila told Max. "She's done a lot of things to help me move ahead, even though my move to corporate R&D will create a headache for her." This type of trust is not the product of a single high-minded act, but is characterized by a pattern of helping worthy subordinates expand their horizons and careers. It must be built over time through consultation, useful coaching, and providing opportunities for the person to move ahead.

- Expertise in the matter at hand. For example, the person you are coaching with sales techniques will trust you *if* you have a reputation as a successful salesperson.

- Being as good as your word. Trust is built through repeated demonstrations that you are worthy of trust. So, whenever you say, "Here's the plan: I'll do X and you will do Y," be sure to hold up your end of the bargain. And do it every time.

- Not disclosing information held in confidence. Discussions with an employee about a performance problem may inadvertently dredge up personal information that the employee would not want shared. Always respect his or her desire for confidentiality. And by all means, do not pry into the personal lives of your subordinates. If a problem outside work is the source of performance problems, this legitimately concerns you—though indirectly. But instead of prying, create an opportunity for the person to volunteer the information.

Build trust, and your coaching experiences will be more productive.

Accountability for Results

A person who isn't held accountable for results will not take coaching seriously. Thus, the salesperson who doesn't see a connection between performance and a paycheck won't take the boss's sales coaching seriously. The person may politely listen and nod, "Yes, I understand what you mean," but his or her behavior is unlikely to change. Consequently, the outcome of this individual's sales work will not change.

If you have a formal coaching plan, that plan should make accountability explicit. "I agree to help you develop your selling skills, and you agree to learn and apply them to produce higher sales." Whenever feasible, express this accountability in measurable quantities: for example, the number of sales contacts made each day, or the time required to process an insurance application. Improvements made in some tasks are less easily quantified, such as the conciseness and readability of a technical report or the quality of a presentation to the company sales force. Even so, a sharp manager can rate the before- and after-coaching quality of these types of tasks.

Motivation to Learn and Improve

Smart parents know that the best time to help their children master a new skill—be it riding a bicycle or tying their shoes—is when children are truly motivated to learn. Either because of peer pressure or because of genuine interest in mastering things that older children do, there comes a time when a child is both physically ready and mentally eager to learn particular skills. Attempts to teach a youngster these new skills before then usually fail. The workplace situation is very similar: coaching coupled with a motivation to learn is a powerful combination. Absent that motivation, coaching efforts are much less effective.

You are probably already familiar with the workplace motivations that encourage people to learn and improve:

- Mastering an important skill will open the door to advancement.

- An employee sees that improved productivity is reflected in her paycheck.

- A person knows that his job is in danger unless he learns to do a particular task better.

- Peer pressure encourages everyone to do his or her best.

- An employee has reached the point where she is eager to learn something new or move on to a more challenging job.

These are the situations in which your coaching will be most effective and most appreciated.

Mutual trust, accountability for results, motivation to learn and improve—create a climate in which these qualities are present, and your coaching, and most of your other managerial activities, will surely be more effective. Are any of these qualities absent from your current coaching relationships?

Avoid These Common Mistakes

Few managers are great coaches. This observation should surprise no one, since so few managers are given any formal instruction in, or other guidance on, coaching methods—either in school or by their own bosses or companies. That lack of training leads to several common mistakes:

1. **Talking too much.** Some managers talk and direct too much and listen too little. Because coaching is a collaborative activity, the coachees must have an opportunity to talk about their work, where they are having problems, how they feel about their abilities, and so forth. A coach learns none of this when dominating the conversation.

   Remedy: Resist the urge to talk, to tell, to direct in the early phase of coaching. When you do talk, ask probing questions like "What is holding you back?" or "How do you usually handle this task?" Alternatively, direct the conversation into an area where more information is needed for diagnosis, for example, "If you don't feel that you have enough time to develop these reports each month, tell me how you're using your time."

2. **Failing to listen.** Getting the employee talking won't do much good if you fail to listen. Listening helps us understand. Many people appear to be listening. They maintain eye contact and keep their mouths shut. But they aren't really processing what they hear or looking for the emotions behind the other person's words. Instead, they are mentally forming their next speech.

   Remedy: Put all other thoughts out of your head as the other person speaks. Concentrate on what that person is telling you.

3. **Losing control of your emotions.** "Damn it, Kowalski," the boss fumed as he pounded his fist on the desk, "how many times do I have to show you how to do this?" Tantrums undermine coaching. They destroy trust and create either fear or hostility

in the subordinate. The only emotions that matter in coaching are those that support the coachee and make him or her more receptive to learning and improvement.

Remedy: Check your emotions at the door. If you are having a bad day or if you are upset by something, postpone your coaching session to another day.

4. **Directing the subordinate toward something he or she will resist without emotional preparation.** Chances are that you will encourage your subordinate to try something new or to reach for something higher, such as giving a presentation in front of an important client or group of senior managers. Encouraging people to stretch is a good thing. If the person lacks confidence or is somehow emotionally unprepared for that step, however, your encouragement will be a wasted effort.

Remedy: You don't have to be a psychologist to be a coach, but sometimes you must practice some psychology to be successful. This goes back to what we said earlier about goals. You should understand the people who work for you—their personal aspirations, capabilities, and even their fears. If you truly understand your employees, then you can prepare them for the things you want them to do. If, for example, lack of self-confidence is an impediment to progress, deal with that fundamental problem before you coach the person on making a group presentation.

In amateur tennis and many other games, you are likely to win if you simply avoid making mistakes. The same holds true in the game of coaching. Avoid the mistakes described above, and your coaching efforts will probably bear fruit. (See "Be a Good Role Model.")

The Challenge of Team Coaching

If your company is like others, many tasks are being handled through teams. Some teams are formed around routine business processes. A

Be a Good Role Model

Remarkably, the ultimate weapon in coaching may be your own on-the-job behavior. Your subordinates are watching you. They observe how you delegate tasks, how you communicate with the group, how you handle your time, and your personal approach to continual learning and improvement. And some subordinates pattern their own behavior on yours. So, if you want to be a great coach, be a great manager and colleague. Set standards of behavior and performance you would want your subordinates to adopt.

bank, for example, may form a team to handle sizable commercial loan applications. That team may include a sales-oriented loan officer, a credit analyst, and clerical personnel trained in producing loan documents. A team like this is usually permanent. Its members jointly plan their production levels and work schedules and may even have responsibility for retaining or rejecting people from the team. Other teams are formed around temporary or infrequent tasks, such as the development of a new product or planning the company's move to a new office building. This type of team brings together cross-functional skills and disbands once its work is done.

Whether the teams are permanent or temporary, the traditional boss-subordinate rules are suspended within teams—the reason is that you cannot obtain the benefits of a team and still have a traditional boss. A team has a leader, but the team leader is not the boss. He or she does not have the usual authority over others and may even be outranked by certain members of the team. Nevertheless, the team leader retains coaching responsibilities.

In his book on team-based work, J. Richard Hackman explains that good coaching helps teams in three ways: first, by enhancing the level of effort that individual members apply to their work; second, by assuring that the work done is appropriate; and third, by helping members make the most of their talents.[1] Good team leaders find coaching opportunities in the course of everyday business. Their coaching can help members with many routine activities: making better presentations, scheduling their work, dealing with intrateam conflict, obtaining external resources, setting up a budget, and even working effectively in a team environment.

Coaching opportunities are especially prevalent within teams because so many of the skills members eventually need are skills they must learn as their projects unfold. For example, an engineer recruited because of her technical capabilities may suddenly find that she must prepare and present a businesslike progress report to the sponsor and senior management. This type of presentation is outside her set of skills and experiences. She must develop presentation skills quickly—and coaching by the leader is often the best solution.

If you are a team leader, you can use coaching to help your colleagues accomplish the following tasks:

- Get back on track when they are having performance problems

- Maximize individual strengths (e.g., build on analytical skills)

- Overcome personal obstacles (e.g., reduce a fear of dealing directly with a difficult team member)

- Achieve new skills and competencies (e.g., learn how to make a better stand-up presentation)

- Prepare for new responsibilities (e.g., take charge of an ad hoc task force)

- Manage themselves more effectively (e.g., improved time management)

As in nonteam environments, good coaching within a team enhances job satisfaction and motivation. It may also improve your working relationship with other team members, making your job as team leader much easier and more successful. Just remember that effective coaching requires mutual agreement. The other person must *want* to do better and must *welcome* your help.

Summing Up

- Be very judicious in the amount of time you allocate to coaching. In some instances, you can delegate particular coaching jobs to others.

- Pay attention to the psychosocial climate in which coaching takes place. The results of coaching generally improve when executives, managers, and supervisors create a climate characterized by mutual trust, accountability for results, and the motivation to learn and improve.

- Avoid common mistakes, and your coaching will improve. Common mistakes include talking too much, failing to listen, losing control of your emotions, and failing to emotionally prepare the coachee for what you want him or her to do.

- Team leaders are not traditional bosses, but they can—and often must—coach their teammates.

- Like everything else, coaching skills improve with practice. So, take every opportunity to practice.

6

Formal Performance Appraisal

Improving Results Through Feedback

Key Topics Covered in This Chapter

- *Appraisal as part of a system of performance management*

- *360-degree feedback and its value*

- *The eight steps of performance appraisal*

HOW WELL ARE your people doing their jobs? Are some falling short of the mark? If they are, do you understand why? Do they understand why? Are they even aware that their work isn't meeting expectations? Others are probably doing just fine—perhaps exceeding expectations. Do you officially note, compliment, and encourage their good work?

Many companies use annual performance appraisals to evaluate how people are doing. Appraisal is one part—but an important part—of the larger system of performance management. This chapter will show you how to handle performance appraisals and will offer eight steps for doing it right. Performance appraisal is a hot topic; some people think that it's a big time-waster, while others swear by it. So, we'll also look at arguments in favor of appraisal and against it.

What Is It?

Performance appraisal is a formal method for assessing how well an individual employee is doing with respect to assigned goals. Its ultimate purpose is to communicate personal goals, motivate good performance, provide constructive feedback, and set the stage for an effective development plan.

Performance appraisal is generally conducted annually, with follow-ups as needed. Like the physical exam administered by your doctor, this annual checkup gives a manager an opportunity to spot performance problems before they become serious and to encourage the continuation of good work. An appraisal also helps the employee and manager focus on the goals and performance expectations that affect salary, merit increases, and promotions. Appraisal sessions are both a confirmation and a formalization of the ongoing feedback that should be part of every manager–subordinate relationship.

Performance appraisals are not widely popular. Star performers look forward to an appraisal because they know that they'll get positive strokes from their bosses. "Well, Ms. Abercrombie, as usual you've met or exceeded all of your goals. I just wish that we had ten more people like you." What's not to like? Other employees approach the appraisal process with apprehension, fearing that they'll get the same report card they received from their eighth-grade teachers: "Dear Mrs. Jones: Jimmy is very bright, but he's not working up to his potential. He needs to work harder on _____." Let's face it, people don't like being told that their work falls short of the mark.

Busy managers are not particularly fond of performance appraisals, either, and generally for two reasons. First, few managers enjoy telling people to their faces that they're not doing their jobs as well as they should. Second, giving performance appraisals to each of many direct reports consumes time—for preparation, administration, documentation, and follow-up. And time is every manager's scarcest asset. Imagine the plight of managers who have ten direct reports. Appraisals for all ten is a hefty time commitment.

Indeed, performance appraisals are usually uncomfortable when an individual isn't doing well, and they definitely take time. But when they are approached with the right frame of mind and done properly, they are worth the effort. When you consider that a manager's fundamental responsibility is to get results *through people,* a systematic approach to assessing the human assets at one's disposal is a must. In addition to providing insights into employee performance, appraisal sessions give the manager opportunities to accomplish other objectives:

- Communicate about goals with their direct reports.

- Increase productivity by providing timely feedback.

- Help the organization make valid decisions about pay, development, and promotions.

- Protect the organization against lawsuits by employees who have been terminated, demoted, or denied a merit increase.

Eight Steps to Effective Appraisal

There is no one right way to conduct performance appraisals. Most companies have a set of suggested procedures, and every subordinate presents a different challenge to the appraising manager. Nevertheless, effective practice generally involves the following eight steps, addressed in this order.

Step 1: Be Prepared

Like every activity, performance appraisal benefits from preparation—by both employees and managers. Little can be accomplished if either the manager or the employee—or both—strolls into an appraisal meeting without having reflected on what has happened during the preceding months.

Let's consider the employee first. It is important to involve an employee in every stage of the appraisal process so that both sides of the story are on the table. One of the best ways of doing this is to have the employee conduct a self-appraisal. In many cases, the human resource department can provide a checklist for this purpose. That checklist states the employee's goals and the job behaviors and functions associated with the goals. (Those goals should have been established with the employee at the very beginning of the appraisal period, as described in chapter 1.)

In self-appraisal, the employee evaluates his or her performance against goals. If your human resource department doesn't provide a self-appraisal checklist, here are a few questions you should ask the employee to address:

- To what extent have you achieved your goals?

- Which, if any, goals have you exceeded?

- Are you currently struggling with any particular goals?

- What is inhibiting your progress toward achieving those goals: lack of training, inadequate resources, poor direction from management, or anything else?

Self-appraisal has two important benefits. First, it gets the employee involved. This involvement sets a tone of partnership for the appraisal process and makes the employee more open to subsequent feedback by the manager. Second, self-appraisal gives the manager a different perspective on the subordinate's work and any related problems. The manager may, in fact, be seeing just a small part of what the employee is doing or struggles with every day.

As manager, you too must appraise your subordinate's performance in relation to the goals set down and explained at an earlier date. In doing this, you can use the same methods described in chapter 3 to identify gaps between goals and performance. Some companies supplement the manager's observations with those of the employee's coworkers, peers, and others with whom he or she interacts in the workplace. These supplementary observations are referred to as *360-degree feedback*. The goal is to determine what it is like working for or with the person, and to isolate his or her strengths and weaknesses.

This type of broadband feedback is very useful. Instead of one person with a unique perspective assessing someone, the observations of many people and many perspectives are brought in. For instance, an "internal customer" of the employee and a peer who works on a cross-functional team with the employee might be asked to record their views. If approached seriously and in the right spirit, 360-degree feedback can reduce the chance of a performance misdiagnosis. It also recognizes that modern business is multifaceted, with no one in particular seeing all dimensions of the employee's work. Thus, several people in a position to know are asked to anonymously rate the quality of the subject's work and his or her interactions with them.

As a method, 360-degree feedback is not without drawbacks. First, it is time-consuming. Think for a moment about the many people whom you might be asked to rate in your organization. Your boss. Four or five of your peers. The person who handles your department's expense reimbursements, and so forth. Now, multiply that number by the one hour typically required to make an evaluation. So, what's the result? Eight hours? Ten? And as you might expect, most people are uncomfortable giving a bad report about someone else—even when that person has glaring shortcomings. The reviewers know that a bad report might result in no raise or, worse, dismissal of the other person. And so they pull their punches—which calls into question the validity of this promising approach to appraisal. After all, what do they have to gain by giving a bad mark to someone who doesn't work directly for them?

Sure, this approach is not free of problems. But the same can be said of many other useful business practices. The benefits of 360-degree feedback outweigh the negatives when the following conditions are in place:

- It is used in an environment of trust.

- There is an organizational commitment to performance evaluation.

- Both the people making and the people interpreting the evaluations have received adequate training.

So, don't ignore this methodology. If it's done right, 360-degree feedback provides much more complete information on an employee's work.

Step 2: Conduct the Performance Appraisal Meeting

Many people are anxious about performance appraisal meetings. So, create a tone of partnership from the very beginning. Start by setting the person at ease; don't let him or her feel like a defendant on trial. The annual appraisal should be a positive event, even when improvement is required.

Second, review the purpose of the appraisal and its benefits for both parties. This will psychologically prepare you and the employee and will act as a warm-up for dialogue.

Then, ask the employee to talk about his or her self-appraisal. This will help you understand the employee's point of view and prevent you from controlling too much of the conversation. Listen very carefully to what the person is saying. Don't interrupt until the person has had his or her say. Demonstrate that you are listening by repeating what you've heard: "If I understand you correctly, you feel that you are meeting all goals with respect to the weekly sales reports, but that you're struggling to contact all the key customers you've been assigned. Do I have that right?"

Once the employee has laid all the cards on the table, move on to your appraisal.

Step 3: Identify Both Good and Bad Performance

As you disclose your appraisal, give priority to how the employee's accomplishments compare to agreed-upon goals. For example, if Joan says that her greatest achievement was organizing and chairing a meeting between key customers and your R&D personnel, ask yourself, "Was this one of her goals?" If it was, how close did that performance come to meeting the metrics of that goal? How did she do in relation to her other goals? Look for gaps between actual and expected performance, but also look for areas in which this person has met or exceeded expectations. Remember, appraisal *isn't* strictly about performance problems!

However, if your appraisal has found a gap between the employee's goal and actual performance, make this a focus of your discussion and feedback. As a starting point, identify a larger organizational goal to explain how the employee's goal supports it. People can and do change when they understand the consequences of their behavior and work. For example, you might say something like this:

> *Our department's goal is to resolve all customer warranty problems within one week. That's our contribution to the company's higher goal of creating customer satisfaction and loyalty—both of which assure our future employment and bonuses. We can't accomplish that if any*

team member fails to handle his or her share of customer complaints. Do you see how what we are doing helps the company meet this important goal?

Make sure the employee affirms your statement. Then, move the conversation toward any performance gaps you have identified. If you've done a good job of developing and communicating performance metrics, you'll have a solid basis for that discussion.

Step 4: Find the Root Causes of Performance Gaps

If the employee is falling short of goals, seek the root cause. "Why do you think your sales this year have fallen short of your goal of $2.2 million?" Listen carefully to the response; give your employee the first opportunity to identify the cause. If you don't get adequate information in the reply, probe with other questions if necessary: "Could the problem be that you need more product information or training? Are you not getting sufficient sales support from me or from the home office?"

Keep up this pattern of give-and-take with your employee, and you'll eventually get to the source of the problem. Be aware, however, that sometimes the root source is something outside the worker's direct control. (See "The Work Process May Be the Source of Performance Problems.")

Identifying the root causes of performance gaps will, in most cases, create an atmosphere of objectivity in which both you and your subordinate can contribute in positive ways. You won't be attacking the subordinate, who will feel less on the defensive. Instead, you'll be working together to address "the problem," which may be *outside* the subordinate's control (e.g., lack of proper training, too few resources, and the workplace environment). The following suggestions can help you offer more useful feedback:

- Encourage the employee to articulate points of disagreement. Again, create an opportunity to get his or her view on the table.

The Work Process May Be the Source of Performance Problems

As you look for root causes of poor performance, don't rule out the possibility that the work processes and tools that your people have been told to use are at fault. Even a talented and committed person will perform poorly if forced to use shoddy tools or a flawed work process. The late W. Edwards Deming, one of the founders of the quality movement, believed that work processes are the root cause of most mistakes and inefficiencies. Work processes, he maintained, are something that management, and not workers, controls.

- Avoid generalizations such as "You just don't seem involved with your work" in favor of specific comments that relate to the job. For example, "I have noticed that you haven't offered any suggestions at our service improvement meetings. Why is that?"

- Be selective. You don't need to recite every shortcoming or failing. Stick to the issues that really matter.

- Give authentic praise as well as meaningful criticism.

- Orient feedback toward problem solving and action.

We've focused on performance problems here. But don't forget to do something similar for performance achievements. Ask the employee to explain how he or she managed to do a task so well. You'll want to encourage this person to keep on that course! There is also a chance that the employee has learned something that can benefit others. So ask, "How did you manage to do that so well?"

Figure 6-1 is a handy checklist that you can use for planning a feedback session. A downloadable version of this checklist and other tools used in the Harvard Business Essentials series can be obtained from the series Web site, www.elearning.hbsp.org/businesstools.

FIGURE 6-1

Planning a feedback session

Name the issue or behavior that needs to be corrected or reinforced.

What is the organizational and personal significance of this issue?

What is the purpose of the feedback?

What details do you have to describe the behavior accurately? (Who, what, when?)

What is the impact of the behavior?

What results do you want to produce?

Who is the best person to give the feedback, and why?

What communication style will be the most effective, and why?

Describe possible barriers to giving this feedback. What can you do to overcome them?

What behavior on the other person's part would be more constructive, and why?

Source: Harvard ManageMentor® on Giving and Receiving Feedback, adapted with permission.

Step 5: Plan to Close Performance Gaps

If you've identified any performance gaps in the previous step and found their root causes, make sure that the employee acknowledges them and their importance. Once that is done, begin a dialogue about their resolution.

Give the employee the first opportunity to develop a plan to close any gaps. Say something like "What would you propose as a solution?" Putting the ball in the employee's court will make him or her more responsible for the solution and, hopefully, more committed to it. As the employee describes a plan to close any gaps, challenge any assumptions and offer ideas for strengthening that plan. If the employee cannot put a credible plan together, you'll have to take a more active approach. In either case, seek from the employee agreement on, and commitment to, the plan. A good plan includes these components:

- Specific goals

- A timeline

- Action steps

- A description of the training, coaching, or practice required, if any

The development plan should become part of the employee's record.

If you cannot settle the matter of closing performance gaps during your appraisal meeting, establish a time and place for a follow-up meeting, and explain its purpose. "Over the next week, I'd like you to think about the things we've discussed today. I'll do the same. We'll then meet again and develop a plan for getting the help you need to handle these problems."

Before concluding the meeting, conduct a brief review of what was said and what agreements were made. This measure makes sure there is no misunderstanding about what both you and your subordinate have taken from the meeting.

Step 6: Reevaluate Performance Goals

Since an entire year may have passed since your subordinates' last formal performance appraisals, reexamine the goals toward which your employees are expected to work. This is especially important when the organization is in a state of change, and when a subordinate is on a rapid trajectory toward workplace mastery. What goals should the person be pursuing in the months ahead? In some cases, the details of this discussion should be taken up in a subsequent conversation with the employee, marking the beginning of a new performance management cycle.

When that conversation takes place, involve the employee in the goal-changing process to be sure that he or she (1) has the capacity to assume new goals and (2) understands the details and the importance of these goals. Always be very clear about the new goals and how performance against them will be measured. Also, depending on employee skills, this is the time to create a development plan (coaching, training, etc.) for giving the employee the capability required to meet the new goals.

Step 7: Get It on the Record

It's very important to document your meeting, its key points, and its outcomes. This means that you'll need to take rough notes during the meeting and complete them immediately afterward, while your memory is still fresh. Getting it on the record is good for you and for the employee. If either of you disagrees with what was discussed or agreed to during your appraisal, you can check the record. Naturally, this can be very important in subsequent legal disputes. So, make a record that includes the following elements:

- The date

- Key points and phrases used by the employee (not necessarily verbatim), including his or her self-appraisal

- Key points and phrases used by you

- Points of disagreement, if any

- A summary of the development plan

- A summary of agreed-upon next steps

- Performance goals for the coming year

Chances are that your company will require that copies of this record be provided to the employee, to the employee's human resource file, and to your files. Usually, both the manager and the employee are asked to sign the performance appraisal report, and in the United States, the employee has a legal right to append his or her own comments to the report.

Step 8: Follow Up

You should plan on following up every appraisal meeting. The high performers and satisfactory performers will obviously need less follow-up. However, if you've given them new, more demanding goals, you'll want to monitor their progress and determine if they need added training, coaching, or other support.

Employees with performance problems and who have committed to development plans should be more carefully monitored. The monitoring could take the form of follow-up meetings as needed. Here, your goal should be to check for progress against development plans. These meetings represent opportunities for coaching and encouragement by you.

Two Problems to Avoid

In the end, performance appraisal is valuable only if people take it seriously and with thoughtfulness and objectivity. Lacking that, you end up with a bureaucratic exercise that annoys people and eats up their time. Consider the following example.

Writing in the *Harvard Business Review,* Dick Grote cited the case of the U.S. Air Force Research Laboratory in Dayton, Ohio. Lab managers conducted annual reviews of their 3,200 scientists and engineers. "They found that nearly all the appraisals were positive—not a single person had been rated 'unsatisfactory,' and only one had been rated 'marginal,'" wrote Grote. "Clearly, such uniformly glowing appraisals are useless in evaluating the relative merits of staff members."[1] Let's face it, many managers are inclined to err in favor of the employee when making an appraisal. The result is a general "performance inflation" in which almost everyone is rated above average—a statistical impossibility. This is a common problem, but does not mean that performance appraisal should be tossed out. It simply means that managers must learn—or be trained—to handle the evaluation more rigorously.

Another problem with formal appraisal is that managers are not particularly good at assessing performance against goals. Sure, if the goal is to assemble 150 personal computers from off-the-shelf parts, or generate mortgage loans equal to $3.5 million, anyone who can count can make an accurate assessment. But few jobs are that clear-cut. The result is that subjective judgment creeps in. Attempts to hand out individual appraisals to ten to fifteen direct reports are inevitably colored by personality, emotions, and selective memory. Consider these problems:

- The manager sees only part of the employee's work activity over the course of the year. Often, an employee's coworkers and internal or external customers know a lot more about the person's performance than the manager does—they observe that performance every day.

- Because the employee's performance in the last month or so is fresh in the manager's mind, it contributes more heavily to the appraisal than it should. The employee's one big mistake or one big contribution over the course of the year sticks in the mind of the manager, outweighing everything else.

Do these problems sound familiar? If they do, here are two things you can do to avoid them:

- Do not rely entirely on your own observations. Seek input from others with whom your subordinate regularly interacts (see the earlier discussion of 360-degree feedback).

- Keep a performance notebook or computer file on each of your direct reports. Update it regularly, and review it prior to your next appraisal meeting. Doing this will solve the problem of selective memory.

Above all, approach performance appraisal with a positive spirit—not as yet another bureaucratic hoop that you and your employees must jump through every year, but as an opportunity to communicate about goals, identify and correct problems, and seek opportunities for better performance. Like every other interpersonal activity, we can get no more out of performance appraisal than we put into it.

Summing Up

- Performance appraisal is a formal method for assessing how well people are doing with respect to their assigned goals. You and your company need these assessments when you make decisions on pay and promotion.

- The eight steps of effective appraisal are (1) preparation, (2) the appraisal meeting, (3) identifying both good and bad performance, (4) finding the root causes of performance gaps, (5) planning how the gaps will be closed, (6) reevaluating goals, (7) documenting your meeting, and (8) follow-up.

- Managers use 360-degree feedback for bringing the observations of many people and perspectives to performance appraisal. This method typically solicits input from internal customers, peers, and work-team members.

7

Employee Development

Helping People Grow in Their Careers

Key Topics Covered in This Chapter

- *The purpose and value of developing employee skills and careers*

- *Where to start*

- *Four tactics for doing it well*

SOME MANAGERS ARE not very good at developing the capabilities of their subordinates. Either they don't think of development as part of their job, or they forget about it in the crush of ongoing business. In both cases, they miss opportunities to build the productive assets of the human resources at their command—a major oversight. Since the job of managers is to produce results through people, doesn't it make sense to increase the productive capabilities of employees? Consider this example:

> Julia does a good job, but her capabilities are limited to the few things she was initially trained to do: file copies of sales invoices and customer correspondence to their respective account folders, and then send those folders to the company's salespeople a week in advance of their scheduled visits to those accounts. She has been doing this work for two years, but her boss, Trish, has so far done nothing to develop Julia's capabilities. If you asked Trish why not, she would say something like this: "I need someone I can count on to manage those account folders, and Julia can do the job. She has her hands full doing that. Why would I want her to do anything else? Besides, I'm too busy to train her."

There are two things wrong with this manager's thinking. First, Julia probably learned just about everything she needed to know about her job within the first few months. She has been on autopilot ever since. This means that she's probably bored, unmotivated, and liable to leave for more interesting or challenging work elsewhere—leaving Trish holding the bag. Second, having mastered her limited job long ago, Julia can probably do the work in her sleep. This means that she can take on other, larger responsibilities—but only if Trish gives Julia permission and training support.

Are you like Trish? If you are, you are standing in the way of skill and career development for your subordinates. You are also demotivating them. Moreover, you are not doing your own career a favor. Here are two reasons why:

1. Managers who haven't developed their subordinates to step into their shoes are less likely to be promoted.

2. Talented and ambitious subordinates will bail out if their career development is stymied, leaving the less talented to do the work.

Managers who take employee development seriously, in contrast, are more likely to attract good people, to produce a workplace with high morale and high standards, and to maintain a spirit of continuous improvement. That's good for employees *and* good for their managers. This chapter offers practical ideas for developing the capabilities of your subordinates.

Begin with the Employee

Development begins with understanding an employee's aspirations and current state of workplace know-how. The more you know about the people who work for you, the more you'll be able to motivate them, coach them, and help them grow. The performance appraisal meeting described in chapter 6 provides one of many opportunities to gain this understanding. If you've prepared for that meeting, you already have a good assessment of the employee's performance. Discussion around that performance—and the person's current goals—should naturally lead to dialogue involving the person's career aspirations and motivation. Let's revisit Trish and Julia to see how Trish might direct the conversation to learn of her subordinate's ambitions and motivation. Trish now understands that employee development is a good thing, and part of her job as supervisor.

Trish and Julia were near the end of Julia's annual performance appraisal session. They had already discussed Julia's current work and the goals Trish wanted Julia to work toward over the next six months. "At this point," said Trish, "I'd like to switch gears away from your current work—which is very satisfactory—to ways you might contribute in the future."

"How do you mean?" Julia responded.

"Well, Julia, you've been doing a good job keeping up the account files for our Southeast District salespeople. In fact, you have it down pat! I'd like to know if you'd be interested in expanding your job in some way—to make your work more challenging and interesting."

"Yes," Julia said, "I'd be open to that. The truth is that after two years, the work has become routine. And just continuing to do the same job won't get me anywhere in the company. It's not that I don't enjoy the work, but I'm not learning anything new."

"That's exactly my concern," said her boss. "Do you have any ideas about how we might alter your job to provide more learning and growth? I have some ideas of my own, but I'd like to hear yours first."

Julia thought on that for a bit. The question was unexpected. "Well, I've been working here in the home office for our eight sales reps in the Southeast District for the past two years, but I'm not very clear on what they do, the problems they have, or the information they need. I just keep their account folders up-to-date. Perhaps if I understood their work better, I could do more to help them."

"So, if I understand you, you see our salespeople as your customers, and you'd like to learn more about them and their needs?"

"That's right."

Trish was pleased by what Julia was saying. Her subordinate obviously was motivated to learn more and to contribute in a larger way. "Let's do this," Trish suggested. "Let's meet at four o'clock next Friday. Between now and then, I'll talk with the HR people and with Bill

Simpson, the Southeast District sales manager, and I'll have some ideas we can discuss."

"I'll look forward to it," said Julia. "And thanks for bringing it up. This has been on my mind for a while."

Develop a Plan

Once you've determined that your subordinate is motivated to gain new skills, the next step is to develop a plan—one that serves that person's aspirations *and* the larger interests of the company. What avenues for learning and job enhancement are available? Perhaps you know the answer from experience. Perhaps the human resource department can help. The plan might involve adding one or two challenging assignments and then using coaching or formal skill training to help the employee achieve them. The right approach will be determined by the employee's situation. Whatever you do, wrap it up in a plan that is challenging yet achievable. Then be prepared to discuss it with the employee, make sensible adjustments, and gain that person's commitment to the plan. Let's return to Trish and Julia, who are meeting again.

"Julia," Trish began, "I spoke with the HR department and with Bill Simpson about your interest in taking on some new challenges this year. My objective was to develop a plan that you would find both challenging and interesting and that would allow you to contribute to our goals at a higher level. Are you still interested?"

"Oh, definitely," she replied.

"I just want you to know that the plan I've developed isn't written in stone. We can make changes. It should be, after all, your plan. In fact, you have no obligation to accept it. You can, if you wish, stick to your regular tasks, which you perform very well."

"I understand. What is your plan?"

"Well," Trish continued, "Bill and I both agree that you will be able to serve your customers—the field sales representatives—better if

you know more about what they do every day. So, we'd like to fly you down to Charleston next month to attend the district midyear sales meeting. You'll get better acquainted with the salespeople, learn a lot about our new products, and, we hope, gain some insights about the support our field reps need from this office. And I can guarantee that you'll have a good time. Bill's meetings are always fun. Does that sound interesting so far?"

"Oh, yes. I'd like to do that."

"Bill also suggested that you tag along with Brenda Jenkins for a day or two when she makes her sales calls in Gainesville, Florida, in September. That will give you some exposure to our customers and how our salespeople operate in the field. Does that sound reasonable?"

"That would be wonderful," said Julia, obviously pleased with the opportunity to get out of the office and learn something new. "But in terms of new duties, what will you want me to do when I get back from these trips?"

"Let's not even try to answer that question yet. We'll meet again after your return from Gainesville. Perhaps you can define some new tasks."

Notice in this story how three elements come together to support employee development: a motivated employee, organizational resources, and support from Trish, Julia's manager. As you work with your subordinates, keep these three elements in mind. It is too soon to tell how Trish's plan will enhance Julia's contributions to the company, but it is clear that the manager's plan will open doors for a valued employee.

Basic Tactics for Employee Development

Trish's plan to provide new learning opportunities for Julia is just one of many tactics that managers can use to develop and motivate their subordinates. In this section, we'll examine several other tactics: job redesign, delegation, skill training, and more general career development.

Job Redesign

If you believe that a subordinate can contribute at a higher level, don't simply pile on new responsibilities. Doing so will lead to employee burnout. Instead, redesign the job at the margins, reassigning rote, lower-level tasks to employees for whom those tasks are more appropriate. Replace those rote tasks with higher-level ones that involve challenge and learning.

The starting point for redesign is a careful inventory of all the tasks associated with the job. These tasks may be found in the formal job description or in your performance appraisal notes. Once you have that list, look for opportunities to offload low-level tasks. Also consider eliminating these tasks altogether; just because someone has always done some task doesn't mean that it is worth doing! Then identify and add a more challenging activity in its place as a regular part of the job.

Task Delegation

Job redesign shifts the job in a permanent way. In some cases, a permanent change may be inappropriate; you may simply want to give your subordinate periodic assignments that provide challenge and experience. Task delegation is a proven managerial mechanism for doing this.

Delegation is the assignment of a specific task or project by one person to another. When you delegate, you transfer not only the work to another person, but also the accountability for completing the work to stated standards. Delegation is one of the most important skills demonstrated by successful managers.

Effective delegation can have real benefits for you, your subordinates, and your organization. Let's start with you. When you delegate a task, you reduce your workload and stress level by removing an item from your to-do list. This gives you more time to focus on activities that require your unique skills and authority: planning, business analysis, controlling operations, obtaining resources, and dealing with people issues. Delegating also improves the level of trust between you and your staff. To gain trust, you must first give trust, and delegating is one way to do it. The message in delegation is "*I trust you* to get the job done."

Good employees likewise benefit from the delegation of tasks and projects. This is where the developmental issue comes in. Every time you delegate an assignment, you're giving someone an opportunity to learn how to accept responsibility, to plan work, and to enlist the collaboration of others. In effect, delegating gives employees experience with managerial work. Consider this example:

> *Bill Simpson, the Southeast District sales manager, was impressed by the performance of Brenda Jenkins, one of the field sales reps under his management. Brenda had been with the company for only four years, but she had already established a fine sales record. She was effective, mature, and ambitious.*
>
> *"When I see someone like that," Bill told one of his peers, "I like to give her as long a leash as she can handle." And he followed through with that philosophy. With the summer sales meeting just four months away, he approached Brenda with the idea of delegating meeting preparations to her.*
>
> *"Brenda," he said over the telephone. "You're doing a terrific job down there in Florida, and I was wondering if you'd consider taking on a short-term assignment for me—one that will broaden your experience and develop your managerial skills."*
>
> *Brenda liked what her boss was saying, and was curious about what would follow. "Of course, I'm always eager to do more," she replied. "What specifically do you have in mind?"*
>
> *"Well," Bill continued, "I've been organizing our district's midyear meetings ever since I took this job six years ago. It's time to get someone else involved—someone with new ideas and who can pep things up. You're that person, Brenda."*
>
> *"I'm flattered that you would trust me with something this important. What's involved?"*
>
> *"Well, I'd expect you to pick a resort hotel with adequate meeting facilities for our group. You'd also arrange for meals and transportation, and recruit an interesting speaker for our wrap-up dinner. Naturally, I'll give you a budget and help you out if you get stuck."*

Being an ambitious person, Brenda agreed to take on the assignment. She saw it as a good learning opportunity and one that would position her for advancement to sales management in the future.

Delegating, as in Brenda's case, is a good way to build the capacities of your people. But be sure to monitor the delegated person's progress, giving feedback and coaching as needed.

Skill Training

Skill training is another method of employee development. It has two aims:

1. To keep the skills of employees current with advancing technologies and business practices

2. To help employees master the skills they need to make greater contributions and to advance within the company

Skill training is a mutually beneficial arrangement. A unit or company that provides effective skill training gains the benefit of workers who are well versed in current standards. And employees benefit by maintaining their "employability" and, in some cases, advancing to higher levels.

Skill training can be either informal or formal. Informal training is generally conducted as on-the-job training, or OJT. This is the least costly form of training, as it doesn't take the employee out of production and is the most prevalent approach to skill development applied by U.S. companies.

Generally, OJT practices in the United States are very unstructured and involve neither designated trainers nor training materials. Japanese companies, in contrast, take a more structured and planned approach to OJT since they consider it a key element of training systems that aim to develop employee competencies over long careers. Clair Brown and Michael Reich describe the Japanese attitude toward OJT:

In Japan, OJT is as carefully planned, mapped, and recorded as company-provided classroom training. Training and skill development are

an expected part of every worker's job. Each employee, from new hire to senior manager, simultaneously thinks of himself as a teacher of the person(s) below him as well as a student of the person who is above. Training the person to take your place is as important as training to move up the job ladder.[1]

Formal training, as practiced by U.S. companies, is more highly structured than OJT and takes place in classroom or "e-learning" settings. It can be used to address both company-specific and general (transferable) skills. Formal training is more expensive than OJT because it takes employees away from their work, makes use of dedicated trainers, and depends on curriculum materials that must be developed and kept up-to-date.

Formal training at many large corporations is dispensed through "corporate universities," of which there are approximately 1,600 in U.S. firms. Jeanne Meister has studied these corporate institutions and points to two reasons for their popularity:[2]

- **They align employee training with business strategy.** By controlling the curriculum, the firm can focus training on the specific skills that complement its strategy. This reduces the problem of skill shortages in key positions.

- **They assure a continual upgrade of internal knowledge.** "Professional knowledge," according to Meister, "is like a carton of milk—it has a shelf life. If you're not replacing everything you know every couple of years, your career is going to turn sour."

Some firms outsource some or all of their skill training to local educational institutions, particularly vocational-technical schools. In areas where these firms are dominant employers, the firms often have a significant say in the curricula of these institutions—and are thus able to shape the training they need for their employees.

Does training pay? Yes and no. When training is on the right skills—those that serve business goals—and done effectively, it is hugely positive. When it is not, it can be costly and unproductive.

Career Development

Career development is an umbrella term that describes the many training experiences, work assignments, and mentoring relationships that move people ahead in their vocations. (See "Tips for Career Development" for a summary of the tips outlined in this section.) Any company that aims to retain valuable people and to fill vacancies caused by retirements, defections, and growth must practice some form of career development. Ultimately, this practice can create a strong "bench" of people who will one day lead the company as technical professionals, managers, and senior executives.

Human resource people often refer to *career ladders* when they talk about career development. A career ladder is a logical series of stages that move a talented and promotable employee through progressively more challenging and responsible positions. For example, in the publishing business, a person with senior editorial aspirations might be progressively moved through various positions in production or marketing to editorial assistant to editor. Each step would broaden his or her skills and understanding of the business.

Some firms systematically analyze a person's current level of skills and experience and match those against the skills and experiences

---

Tips for Career Development

- Provide a career ladder for every subordinate you value.

- For promotable individuals, identify gaps between the skills and experience they now have and those they'll need to step into new roles. Then, fill those gaps with training and appropriate assignments.

- Don't allow good people to get stuck on career plateaus.

- Make sure that everyone who needs one has a suitable mentor.

needed at the next step up the ladder. Gaps between what the person has and what he or she needs are then addressed through a plan that involves some combination of formal training, special assignments, and regular mentoring by a respected superior, as depicted in figure 7-1.

From a retention perspective, the career ladder approach is most effective when it eliminates plateaus. The employee should always feel that he or she is learning and being challenged with a manageable new set of responsibilities. There should be plenty of excitement and no chance of feeling stuck on a career plateau. That "stuck" feeling demotivates and creates the potential for defection. If circumstances bar a promising employee's vertical advancement for the future, the manager should find some type of lateral assignment that will engage the employee's interest and provide learning experiences.

Now, ask yourself these questions about career ladders in your unit:

- What career ladders are available to my valued employees right now?

- Are my people aware of those ladders and taking advantage of them?

- Have I identified and made provisions for the skills and experiences that my charges will need to climb to the next level?

- Who, if anyone, is currently stuck on a plateau? What can be done to get him or her off the plateau?

FIGURE 7-1

Filling skill and experience gaps

Source: Hiring and Keeping the Best People, Harvard Business Essentials series (Boston: Harvard Business School Press, 2003).

As a manager, you have the responsibility of making sure that the people you value are on progressively advancing career paths. Their progress is also good for you since it will be easier for you to move up if you've developed a successor capable of stepping into your shoes.

Summing Up

- Employee development begins with an understanding of an employee's current state of workplace know-how and performance, aspirations, and motivation.

- Once you've determined that your subordinate is motivated to gain new skills, the next step is to develop a plan—one that serves the person's aspirations *and* the larger interests of the company.

- Three elements that support employee development are employee motivation, organizational resources (through training), and a supportive manager.

- The basic tactics of employee development include job redesign, task delegation, skill training, and career development.

8

Intractable Performance Problems

Face Them Head-On

Key Topics Covered in This Chapter

- *A two-step process for dealing with poor performance*

- *The best ways to handle C-level performers*

- *When dismissal is the best course*

PROBLEM EMPLOYEES. Their performance or workplace behavior is unsatisfactory. They show little commitment to the job and appear bored. Employee entitlements interest them more than their goals. Counseling sessions always end the same way: these employees agree to change but do not follow through. Worse, they eat up your time and create dissatisfaction among their colleagues. And they put your managerial ability to the test. Do you have subordinates like these?

This chapter examines the problems that managers encounter in dealing with subordinates who have performance problems that have not responded to coaching and other interventions. It also considers what to do with burnout cases, whose normally good performance has changed for the worse, and C-level performers.

Diagnose the Problem

The first step in dealing with repeated poor performance is to diagnose the problem. You want to be *very* sure that your concerns are based on solid facts. Moreover, you don't want to be making a mountain out of a molehill. In your diagnosis, follow the same routine we described in chapter 3 on identifying performance gaps:

- Observe and gather data.
- Compare what you observe with the employee's performance goals.
- Look for possible causes for the problem: poor job design, conflict with another employee, and so forth.

- As a check on your own observations, ask other sources (in confidence) what they've seen. Are their observations the same as yours?

Once you've followed these steps, develop a short, documented list of examples of the repeatedly observed problem, as in the following example:

> Sarah was concerned about the performance of Michael, one of her direct reports. On Tuesday morning, she had asked him for a written report on the status of key customer accounts in his sales territory. Stressing the urgency of her request, she had asked for the report by three o'clock that day. As of Wednesday, Michael hadn't complied.
>
> Sarah was annoyed by Michael's failure to deliver; she was also concerned with what seemed to be a pattern. Looking back in her records, she noted that Michael's reports were often either late or incomplete. His last annual performance review cited the same problem.
>
> Using her records and her own recollection of events, Sarah summarized Michael's recent performance in the area of reports in a short list. She would use that list later, when she spoke with Michael about the problem.

The purpose of diagnosis is to pinpoint and document the problem. Do this, and you'll be prepared for the next step.

Confront Poor Performers

The next step is to confront the employee with the facts. Then, provide frank and honest feedback about the problem you see. Feedback gives each party an opportunity to tell his or her side and to hear the same from the other. Here are nine tips for using the feedback approach:

1. Make sure that work expectations and performance objectives are clear. The only way to verify the existence of a performance problem is to state the expected level of performance and to measure the employee's actual performance against it.

2. If you've completed the diagnosis step, you have all the details. Review these details with the employee. Don't try to wing it or to describe the problem in general terms.

3. Give the person advance notice, and specify the issue of concern. For example, for a person who is chronically late for work, you might say, "I'd like to speak with you tomorrow about work hours. Please come prepared to discuss your starting time."

4. When your meeting date finally arrives, describe the problematic behavior and its impact on you and on others. For example, "You've been coming to work a half-hour late several days each week for the past month. I recognize that you make up the missed time by either staying late or working through lunch, but that's not a solution. Because we operate in teams, having one person unavailable can mess up the work that three or four others are doing."

5. Refer to the context of the problem. "This is not the first time we've had to talk about this. According to my records, we discussed this problem six weeks ago and again last December. Yet the problem continues."

6. Listen actively to the employee's response. Don't get distracted with thinking about what you'll say next. Be open to what the person says.

7. Make a suggestion or request, and then check for understanding. For example, "What I'd suggest is that you rearrange your activities before work so that you can be punctual. That will make our work around here much easier and make everyone on your team happier. And you and I won't have to have another of these conversations." Then, check for the receiver's understanding of your suggestion: "Do you understand why I'm insisting on your being on time?"

8. Check for agreement or commitment on the next steps. For example, "So, you agree that you'll be here and ready to work at nine o'clock every morning?"

9. Keep a record of what was said and any agreement made. Check to determine if the employee is complying with the agreement.

Keep the Focus on the Future

As you provide feedback, focus on improving future performance. After all, your goal here is to change the person's performance or workplace behavior for the better, not rack someone over the coals.

Also, don't limit feedback to poor performance. If it's justifiable, mix some good news with the bad. It will make the bitter pill of criticism easier to swallow. For example, "I don't like coming down on you about being late to work, because the work you do when you're here is exemplary. The trouble is that you need to start that exemplary work at nine o'clock."

Don't Avoid Confrontation When It's Necessary

If you're like most managers, confronting problem employees in this way and pointing out their shortcomings is the *least* enjoyable part of your job. A trip to the dentist for a tooth filling may be preferable. No one likes to deliver bad news or tell someone that his or her work or behavior is unacceptable. (See "Common Employee Behavior Problems and How to Cure Them" for advice on handling problems with employees whose performance is up to standard but whose behavior can nevertheless be demotivating to others around them.)

Most people are, in fact, conflict avoiders. Still, someone must do it; otherwise, the employee's unacceptable work or behavior will most likely continue—or even get worse.

Here are some things to tell yourself whenever you feel a natural reluctance to confront poor performance:

- **It's my duty to do this.** Think of confronting the poor performer as a test of your fitness for managerial work. If you cannot or will not engage in uncomfortable conversations, then you're in the wrong business.

- **Not doing this will undermine the team.** Poor performers demoralize others and thwart your success and the success of the unit as a whole. You cannot allow one or two people to damage everyone else.

- **I'll be doing that person a favor.** The poor performer may actually think that he or she is doing satisfactory work. A frank discussion will clear up the misconception and give the employee an opportunity to improve, perhaps saving his or her job.

- **It won't kill me.** Having a frank discussion about performance problems isn't fun. It isn't pleasant. But it will be over in twenty to thirty minutes, and life will go on. And such a discussion is much easier to do the second time. (If you have any reason to fear that the other person will react violently to your criticism, have one or two other people, perhaps from human resources, in the room with you.)

Remind yourself of these points, and you will be less reluctant to step up to the problem.

Handling C Performers

As you work to raise the overall performance level of your unit, so-called problem employees should not be your sole concern. There may also be people who, though they are not "failing," are turning in mediocre performance. These too demand your attention.

Every organization has a distribution of performers from the best to average to the worst. On one end of the distribution are the A performers, whose contributions are exceptional. The B performers do very good work and generally form the solid backbone of units and departments. The C performers, on the other hand, do work that is just barely acceptable. In their study of managerial talent in two large companies, Beth Axelrod, Helen Handfield-Jones, and Ed Michaels of McKinsey & Company found that the contributions to profit growth of these A, B, and C groups were miles apart. On average, A managers grew profits 80 percent in one company and 130 percent in the other. C managers in these same companies achieved no profit growth whatsoever. This raises a question about where skill and career development resources should be focused. Certainly, well-managed investments in the development of A

Common Employee Behavior Problems and How to Cure Them

Some workplace behavior can demotivate employees, even though the perpetrators may be performing up to standard.

- **Gossip mongers.** These people enjoy spreading gossip, rumor, and innuendo. It makes them feel influential and gives the appearance that they have inside information. Their behavior unduly upsets people and disrupts the workplace. Explain how gossip and inflammatory rumors can hurt the whole organization. If it's possible, redirect the gossip monger's energy into activities that are more positive.

- **Complainers.** These people find nothing positive to say about their jobs, their bosses, or the company. And they are not shy about sharing their dark views with anyone who will listen. Show some concern that the person isn't happy on the job. Listen to and deal with legitimate complaints. Solicit suggestions for improving the way your team works. But explain firmly that a constant negative attitude will damage team enthusiasm and commitment, and that you will not tolerate a bad attitude.

- **Mean-spirited jokesters.** A little lighthearted banter and kidding can reduce workplace stress and improve morale. But joking that is mean-spirited or done at the expense of particular individuals does the opposite and should not be tolerated. Make it clear that racist, homophobic, sexist, or other offensive comments are unacceptable in the workplace and that people who persist in making these comments or jokes will be disciplined.

SOURCE: Harvard ManageMentor® on Dismissing an Employee, adapted with permission.

and B performers make perfect sense. But what about C performers? Should you invest in their improvement or simply move them out of the way?

Some companies, General Electric being one, regularly prune the ranks of their C-performing managers through a policy of forced ranking that routinely dismisses people in the bottom 10 percent of performance. Other companies try to bring low performers up a notch. But too many organizations do nothing to deal with C performers. The cost of this indifference is high, both in defections by good employees and in lack of profit growth. As the authors write with reference to the managers in their survey:

> *Consider that every C performer fills a role and therefore blocks the advancement and development of other more talented people in an organization. At the same time, C performers usually aren't good role models, coaches, or mentors for others. Eighty percent of respondents in our survey said working for a low performer prevented them from learning, kept them from making greater contributions to the organization, and made them want to leave the company. Imagine, then, the collective impact on the talent pool and morale of a company if just 20 of its managers are underperformers and if each of them manages ten people.*[1]

So, what should be done? Axelrod and her colleagues suggest a three-step approach:

1. Identify your C performers.

2. Agree on explicit action plans for each C performer. Some C players can improve their performance substantially if given the direction and appropriate developmental support.

3. Hold managers and supervisors accountable for the improvement or removal of C performers.

Many C players are not worth keeping, at least not in their current positions. Those who cannot improve after coaching and counseling should be moved into lower-level jobs, where they have the potential to be A or B performers. Failure in those positions should be followed by termination.

Nevertheless, investments in C performers may be worthwhile. The only way to know for sure is to estimate how organizational performance would improve if you could shift a C-level person to the next highest level.

Is Burnout the Problem?

Every once in a while, you'll encounter a poor performer who was once, according to human resource records or your own recollection, an excellent employee. This person is now just going through the motions and getting by. What went wrong? Perhaps you're looking at a case of burnout.

Burnout is work exhaustion. It is sometimes self-induced, but, in many other cases, is a result of the workplace culture. Burnout typically manifests itself through lower job performance and satisfaction, less commitment to the organization, and a heightened intention to "do something different."

Burnout generally results from long-term involvement in situations that have many negative attributes, such as these:

- Work overload

- Conflicting demands (e.g., "Think big and be creative—but don't make any mistakes")

- Monotonous tasks

- Too few rewards (bonuses, extra time off, etc.)

- Little acknowledgment of employee contributions

- A failure to achieve clear success as defined by the employee

As the list indicates, burnout is not strictly a function of the number of working hours. A person may work countless hours and still feel highly motivated. Rather, most people burn out when they feel more stress than support in their work lives. And the worst aspect of this syndrome is that highly competent and committed employees are most susceptible to it.

Managers sometimes contribute to the burnout problem without realizing it. Their natural instinct is to load all the critical projects on to their few top performers. "I can't trust anyone else to do it right," they say in justification. And then, when these workhorses have succeeded with one project, their managers immediately load them up with another! Meanwhile, the lax and the lazy coast along, picking up their paychecks every two weeks. Are the workhorses of the department given promotions for all their good works? Not always. If they were promoted, there would be no one left to handle the important jobs.

Here are a few tactics for combating burnout:

- **Create a long-term staffing plan.** The plan should ensure that your group has enough people—and enough of the right people—to do the job.

- **Consider internal redeployment of personnel.** If you don't repot your houseplants every so often, their roots become impacted and stop growing. The same applies to people. They periodically need new challenges to stay motivated and committed.

- **Provide variety.** Internal redeployment may not be necessary if you can find ways to vary tasks and responsibilities. You might, for example, give one person in your department responsibility for leading a team-based project for the next six months; after six months, rotate the task to someone else. Another person could be given temporary responsibility for facilities maintenance in your work area. Just be sure that those responsibilities are added to the individual's performance objectives and taken seriously. Rather than moving responsibilities around like chess pieces, think about what might be the best opportunities for your people—and emphasize any professional development benefits offered by those opportunities.

- **Regularly monitor workloads.** Regular monitoring is especially important for your top performers. One of the major U.S. accounting firms did this by screening travel schedules. Individuals observed to be spending excessive time on the road or volunteering for too many projects were identified and counseled. If you find people like this, meet with them regularly to see how they're doing. This act alone can help people feel supported. And go a step further—do something about their schedules before the employees flame out.

- **Consider job redesign.** If a valued employee shows symptoms of burnout, take a look at his or her job description. The tasks and responsibilities of the job may be beyond the powers of even an exceptional worker. In these cases, talk with the human resource department and your staff about redesigning the job.

Above all, be a keen observer and a good listener. Acknowledge cries for help—such as "I don't know how I'm going to keep up," "I'm swamped," or "It looks like I'll have to work over the weekend *again*." Then, do something to alleviate the situation.

When All Else Fails

Occasionally, no amount of coaching, extra training, feedback sessions, or haranguing can get an employee's performance up to an acceptable level. Dismissal is generally the only feasible course of action in these cases—one of the most difficult and painful tasks in any manager's work life. Dismissals can be emotionally difficult and, if poorly handled, can negatively affect a company's reputation and lead to lawsuits. They may also destroy trust and morale throughout the unit. Friends and supporters of the former employee may feel angry and disaffected—if not threatened. But remember: those who felt frustrated or annoyed by the dismissed person's poor performance may feel relieved.

Grounds for a Dismissal

Except in cases of layoffs, an individual's dismissal should be a consequence of performance or behavior that is hopelessly problematic, or when an employee violates the law or a company policy (e.g., by stealing or by sexually harassing another employee).

The laws and company policies governing dismissals are complex. Various forms of employee status—such as exempt versus nonexempt, or union versus nonunion—add to this complexity. A general awareness of these implications can guide you when dismissing an employee. However, it's vital that you follow your firm's policies exactly and seek legal advice from your internal or external corporate counsel. Sloppy handling of a dismissal can result in a costly and time-consuming wrongful-dismissal suit, so let your company's legal department guide you every step of the way.

Most managers feel some confusion or uncertainty over how to decide whether to dismiss a worker or how to actually implement a dismissal if matters should come to that. This is natural. Here are some questions that typically come to a manager's mind:

- When is it legal to dismiss someone?

- How and when should I break the news to an affected employee?

- How should I handle the action in terms of legal and company policy?

- How can I preserve morale and trust among the remaining team members, some of whom may question the dismissal decision or may have been friends with the affected employee?

- What's the best way to realign the work roles in the department after the person leaves?

Legal Issues

What constitutes a solid legal reason for dismissing an employee? In some cases, you stand on firm legal ground when you dismiss a worker. In other cases, the situation is murky—and you need to proceed carefully. In the United States, offenses for which immediate dismissal is almost always justifiable include the following:

- Possessing an unapproved weapon at work

- Flagrantly violating the most serious company rules, such as giving away trade secrets to competitors

- Being dishonest about significant workplace issues, such as deliberately and materially falsifying one's travel expenses

- Endangering coworkers' health and safety

- Sexually harassing coworkers or otherwise threatening them in ways that prevent them from doing their work

- Engaging in criminal activity

- Using alcohol or drugs at work

- Gambling on the job

Laws vary from state to state and from nation to nation. So, consult legal counsel to make sure you understand the regulations unique to your situation. (See "When You Cannot Dismiss an Employee.") In U.S. businesses, the following workplace wrongs merit dismissal if they persist or go uncorrected after being brought to the employee's attention:

- Performing poorly on the job

- Refusing to follow instructions

- Having a persistently negative or destructive attitude

- Being insubordinate

- Abusing sick leave and other privileges

- Being chronically late or absent

Whatever your reason for dismissal, it's vital to document the employee's behavior and the steps you've taken to correct it. Being

able to point to a history of problem behavior in documented employee performance reviews, personnel files, memos, and private
notes can be invaluable if a dismissed employee claims that his or her
dismissal was unjustified. So, be sure to document your coaching and
counseling sessions, as well as formal and impromptu appraisal sessions, with a poorly performing employee. The paper trail will be
invaluable if the situation deteriorates to the point of dismissal.

Dismissing an employee is an action you should approach with
great care and usually with the support of human resource professionals and legal counsel. For suggestions on how to break the news
to the employee, conduct a dismissal meeting, and follow up, see appendix B.

Getting On with the Work

After a dismissal, you need to address team members' concerns. You
will also need to redistribute the former employee's work among the
remaining team members and ensure that the former employee's
skills are still represented in the group.

You'll need to notify workers as soon as possible after someone
has been dismissed. Pretending that nothing has happened will only
fuel gossip. One recommended approach is to hold a team meeting
in which you concisely explain what has happened. For example,
you might say, "Toby was dismissed after many months of unsuc-
cessful effort to improve his work performance." Do not go into detail about, or otherwise elaborate on, your decision. Also, be sure not
to criticize the former employee. Then, reassure the team members
that the dismissal had nothing to do with their own performance or
behavior. Acknowledge that this is a difficult time for the entire team
and that you understand that some people will be feeling uncomfortable about it. Then, explain what your plans are for seeking a re-
placement and whether the team's focus will change because of the
employee's departure.

But don't let your communication end there. After the initial
group meeting, spend a little time with each person to listen to any

When You Cannot Dismiss an Employee

There are certain behaviors for which a company *cannot* legally dismiss an employee. These vary from jurisdiction to jurisdiction, but examples include employee behaviors such as these:

- Filing a workers' compensation claim

- Blowing the whistle on illegal behavior on the company's part

- Reporting or complaining about company violations of occupational safety and health laws

- Exercising the right to belong or not to belong to a union

- Taking time off from work to perform a civic duty, such as serving on a jury or voting

- Taking off from work a day that is a holiday under federal or state law

Ask your legal counsel to advise you regarding these regulations. The rules are complicated, so don't try to interpret them on your own.

concerns and to help each individual process his or her feelings about the change.

This chapter has focused on subordinates with serious performance problems. How you deal with the people and the problems says a great deal about your managerial abilities. If you confront problem employees and their problems decisively, you will gain the confidence of both your employees and senior management. And you'll grow stronger from the experience.

Summing Up

- Always begin by diagnosing the problem and preparing a fact-based case.

- Confront the problem employee with the facts. Offer frank and honest feedback about the problem you see.

- Keep the focus of your feedback on the future; your goal is to improve future performance.

- Confronting a problem employee is never pleasant, but don't shrink from the task. It is a test of your fitness for managerial work.

- It is important to help C performers to higher performance levels or to move them to a position in which they can excel.

- Watch for burnout. Are you contributing to it?

Epilogue

What Leaders Must Do

This book has presented a system of performance management. That system provides a set of activities through which managers can make the most of the human resources at their disposal. As described in the preceding chapters, it all begins with goals. Once goals are set and linked to solid metrics, the manager has a practical guide to assessing actual performance. Motivation and coaching are then applied as needed to keep individual employees on track and on their way to superior performance. At some specified date, a formal appraisal is made, the outcome of which is used for decisions on pay, promotions, and employee development—and, in some cases, dismissal. The cycle then begins anew.

It's all very logical. But remember, a system is only as good as the spirit in which people engage it. If managers grudgingly approach performance management as a checklist of chores they must do, appraisal forms they must fill out, and so forth, the system will accomplish less than its potential. In a system like this, we only get out of it what we put into it.

This is where leadership comes into play. When the boss says, "This is important," people take notice. When top management is serious about performance management—and visibly practices it—that sets the tone for the organization. When top management sets high standards of performance and challenges people to excel and improve, it provides an example that managers and employees down the line are likely to follow. Some business leaders have managed to do this exceptionally well. Jack Welch was one such leader. During his tenure as CEO of General Electric, Welch set the tone and the pace of GE with respect to the performance of individual managers. He was a tough character, never accepting second-best from people. He demoted or dismissed managers who didn't meet their goals, but in his view, none of these managers had any reason to be surprised. They always knew where they stood, because Welch gave them regular feedback about their performance. The business culture he produced was tough-minded and performance-oriented, and GE was enormously successful under his watch.

Yes, senior management has the major responsibility for creating expectations and for setting the bar of performance for the entire business. But this shouldn't let other managers off the hook. If you are a middle manager, you have authority and influence within your unit. You cannot change the company, but you can, and should, create high expectations of performance among your peers and subordinates. Do this, and your performance management system will help turn those expectations into reality.

Useful Implementation Tools

This appendix contains two useful items. Both are freely download-able from the Harvard Business Essentials series Web site, www .elearning.hbsp.org/businesstools. Readers can freely access this and other worksheets, checklists, and interactive tools found on that site.

1. **A coach's self-evaluation checklist (figure A-1).** Are you a good coach? Use this checklist to evaluate your coaching skills. If this self-test indicates that you need work in that area, be sure to read the two coaching chapters in this book.

2. **Annual core performance expectations and development plan (figure A-2).** Does your company have a regular format for conducting annual performance appraisals? If it does not, feel free to use or adapt this plan. Chances are that it covers all the points you'd want to address in an employee appraisal.

FIGURE A-1

A coach's self-evaluation checklist

The questions below relate to the skills and qualities needed to be an effective coach. Use this tool to evaluate your own effectiveness as a coach.

Question	Yes	No
1. Do you show interest in career development, not just short-term performance?		
2. Do you provide both support and autonomy?		
3. Do you set high yet attainable goals?		
4. Do you serve as a role model?		
5. Do you communicate business strategies and expected behaviors as a basis for establishing objectives?		
6. Do you work with the individual you are coaching to generate alternative approaches or solutions that you can consider together?		
7. Before giving feedback, do you observe carefully, and without bias, the individual you are coaching?		
8. Do you separate observations from judgments or assumptions?		
9. Do you test your theories about a person's behavior before acting on them?		
10. Are you careful to avoid using your own performance as a yardstick for measuring others?		
11. Do you focus your attention and avoid distractions when someone is talking to you?		
12. Do you paraphrase or otherwise clarify what is being said in a discussion?		
13. Do you use relaxed body language and verbal cues to encourage a speaker during conversations?		
14. Do you use open-ended questions to promote the sharing of ideas and information?		
15. Do you give specific feedback?		
16. Do you give timely feedback?		
17. Do you give feedback that focuses on behavior and its consequences (rather than on vague judgments)?		
18. Do you give positive as well as negative feedback?		
19. Do you try to reach agreement on desired goals and outcomes rather than simply dictate them?		
20. Do you try to prepare for coaching discussions in advance?		
21. Do you always follow up on a coaching discussion to make sure progress is proceeding as planned?		

When you have these characteristics and use these strategies, people trust you and turn to you for both professional and personal support.

If you answered yes to most of these questions, you are probably an effective coach.

If you answered no to some or many of these questions, you may want to consider how you can further develop your coaching skills.

Source: Harvard ManageMentor® on Coaching, adapted with permission.

FIGURE A-2

Annual core performance expectations and development plan

Name _____ Year _____

Supervisor _____ Employee Job title _____

I. Distillation of job description (200 words or less)

II. Measures of core performance (Please add other important job functions, and then check the appropriate box. Add rows as needed.)

Core performance expectations (add rows as needed)	Priority (optional)	Rating			
		Did not meet expectations	Developing	Proficient	Role model
Key functional expectations (4–8 total)					
Managerial responsibilities Conducts interim performance discussions and completes annual assessments on time					
Key behaviors necessary for success (4–8 total)					
Activities to support corporate or unit goals					
Developmental expectations and professional growth[a] (if not included above, add rows as needed) Example: delegates well—minimizes micromanaging. Clarifies roles and responsibilities of direct reports, which allows these people to manage their own work. Defines and communicates appropriate areas of involvement.					

[a] Detailed activities should be specified in an individual development plan.

Employee _____ Date _____

Supervisor _____ Date _____

Continued

III. Leadership Measures					
Core performance expectations (add rows as needed)	**Priority** (optional)	Rating			
		Did not meet expectations	**Developing**	**Proficient**	**Role model**
Sets a clear vision, and drives to it. Guides staff toward clear unit or department expectations. Communicates vision. Identifies and resolves issues. Ensures that staff members understand company and unit direction and are confident in leadership's ability to get there.					
Delivers results. Clarifies measures of success. Organizes work to maximize efficiency and results; holds employees accountable for quality of project completion. Guides staff through appropriate changes; keeps staff informed and develops strategies for dealing with resistance to change.					
Communicates well. Meets with staff regularly. Communicates clear goals and priorities. Identifies and communicates expectations of employees' roles and responsibilities. Demonstrates effectiveness when communicating orally or in writing. Leads meetings effectively. Communicates to clarify direction and build morale.					
Is decisive. Gathers data, analyzes problems, develops solutions, and organizes work. Exercises sound judgment in his or her actions. Gathers input as needed. Demonstrates understanding of when to seek advice in decision making. Communicates decisions.					
Takes risks. Identifies risks of alternative actions. Leads efforts to calculate risk of available options. Identifies ways to mitigate risks. Seeks ways to mitigate risk. Uses good judgment in accepting risk.					
Develops people. Provides guidance and feedback to staff. Aligns opportunities for growth with needed tasks. Creates challenging work assignments. Conducts performance assessment and development plan discussions					

Core performance expectations (add rows as needed)	Priority (optional)	Rating			
		Did not meet expectations	Developing	Proficient	Role model
in a timely manner. Objectively monitors and describes behaviors and their effects. Develops solutions for situations involving performance issues. Demonstrates responsibility for managing morale and retention.					
Serves the mission with humanity. Maintains quality standards in keeping with the brand. Consistently works to improve the practice of management through emotional intelligence.					

Employee _____ **Date** _____

Supervisor _____ **Date** _____

Rating categories

Category	Description
Role model	Consistently displayed behavior that shows mastery of the job function. In addition, the person has exceeded the job expectations and requirements by routinely demonstrating how the job function is used in conducting and sustaining the company's business at all levels. (No more than 20 percent of your employees can receive this rating.)
Proficient	Consistently displayed behavior that shows proficiency (skill and competency) of the job function.
Developing	Displayed behavior that indicates some proficiency (skill and competency); however, this function continues to need full development.
Did not meet expectations	Consistently displayed behavior that is below full job requirements, does not meet expectations, and requires improvement.

IV. Interim discussions (Use as a work in progress to measure performance throughout the year.)

January progress

April progress

July progress

Employee _____ **Date** _____
Supervisor _____ **Date** _____

Handling a Dismissal

Disclaimer: At several points, this appendix refers to legal concerns involved in making and communicating the decision to dismiss an employee. These references are not intended as legal advice. Consult with legal counsel who can advise you on the specifics of your situation.

As we pointed out in the main part of the book, in some cases, performance improvement is not a practical solution and the employee in question must be dismissed. Eventually, most managers run into this situation, and it is important to be prepared. To do it right and in a professional manner, you must do your homework with respect to legal issues and have written documentation of the employee's performance or behavior and the steps you've taken to help. You should feel confident that dismissing the person is the right thing to do—for him or her, for your team, and for your company.

Breaking the News

Once you've done your homework, schedule a meeting with the employee to break the news. Some experts advise against dismissing an employee on a Friday afternoon. A dismissal just before a weekend may cause the person to stew over the weekend and possibly ponder a lawsuit or think about returning to the office with disruptive intentions. So, consider scheduling a meeting on a Monday afternoon.

That way, the employee will have all week to start looking for another job. Whichever day you choose, you'll want to make sure that this day is the person's final day on the job. Most experts advise against allowing a person to remain on the premises for any length of time. Doing so creates discomfort in the workplace and gives a disgruntled individual opportunities to take proprietary files, sabotage computers, and send out nasty e-mails to other employees.

Meet with the employee in a place that keeps both of you out of sight, such as a windowless conference room or office, or some other space that gives you complete privacy. Also, arrange for a path to and from the meeting to avoid areas that are likely to be populated by curious coworkers. Keeping the meeting private shows respect for the affected employee. No one wants to know that his or her coworkers are overhearing or seeing what is bound to feel like a humiliating experience.

To handle the dismissal as effectively as possible, enlist someone from human resources to be present at the meeting. This person can help in the following ways:

- Serve as an impassive voice if you or the employee becomes overly emotional during the meeting.

- Act as a buffer in case of an emotional or a physical outburst from the employee.

- Answer the inevitable questions regarding pensions, insurance, and severance pay.

- Serve as a witness to the conversation in the case of a future dispute.

Get the meeting over with as quickly as possible—in ten minutes or less. Don't allow it to drag on. The more concisely you convey the news to the employee, the less prone you'll be to say something that might expose your company to liability. Be dispassionate, direct, and focused. Convey a sense of serious purpose and resoluteness. To avoid planting the seeds for legal problems, resist the temptation to apologize or to reconsider your decision in light of protests from the employee. The person must know that your decision is final and not subject to negotiation.

So, what should you say? Explain in general terms that the job has not worked out. If you choose to explain in more detail, do so in an objective, neutral tone that doesn't make the employee feel personally attacked. Examples might include the following: "We talked about your not meeting the performance goals for your role six times over the past year. These goals still haven't been met." Or, "You've received coaching and counseling to help you deal with your critical attitude toward colleagues, but your behavior hasn't changed." Citing objective reasons in a neutral tone will lessen the chances that the person will sue or defame you or the company.

Strike a balance between being concise and direct, and being empathetic. That is, do acknowledge that losing a job is likely to have a profound impact on the person's life; for example, "I know this is hard for you." After delivering the news, give the person time to vent his or her anger, confusion, or bitterness for a few moments. Empathy and a chance to process emotions can help people bear difficult news.

Deliver the news in a way that preserves the person's dignity. This includes making arrangements for the employee to remove his or her personal effects from the office during off-hours or over the weekend (with monitoring from someone in the company). Employees who are made to feel humiliated before colleagues or disrespected and personally attacked during a dismissal will be more likely to feel angry and thus desire retribution. Finally, describe whatever severance package, outsourcing assistance, or unused vacation pay is available.

What Not to Say During a Dismissal Meeting

The specific language you use while dismissing an employee can play a major role in whether the person decides to sue. Use the following don'ts as guidelines during a dismissal:

- Don't side with the worker or foster an us-against-them mindset to ease your own discomfort. For example, don't say, "Personally, I don't think that letting you go is the right decision."

- Don't tell a dismissed employee that the dismissal is part of a layoff when it is not. This white lie could come back to haunt you in the form of a discrimination suit if you hire someone new to fill the vacated position.

- Don't say anything like "We're after a more dynamic, aggressive workforce," or "You just don't fit into the team," or "We need people with fewer family commitments who can see clients after normal work hours," or "We need to project a high-energy image." These kinds of statements could give the impression that the employee is being dismissed for discriminatory reasons, such as being too old, foreign, married, and so forth.

- Don't use humor or try to make light of the situation. You'll only make the meeting even more painfully awkward. Worse, you may make the person feel laughed at or humiliated—and therefore more motivated to sue for wrongful dismissal.

- Don't threaten an employee who implies that he or she may challenge the dismissal, for example, by implying that you'll withhold the person's final paycheck unless he or she agrees not to sue. These forms of persuasion are considered illegal coercion and may come back to haunt you in court.

After the Dismissal

Once you have made it through the difficult conversation in which you had to dismiss a problem employee, you will probably feel relieved that the task is over. However, you still have a lot of work to do. In the immediate and longer-term aftermath of a dismissal, you need to take the following steps:

- Ensure that the company and the employee honor any employment contracts—such as noncompete and nondisclosure agreements, a promise to provide service letters, or collective-bargaining agreements.

- Avoid saying anything about the former employee (whether informally or formally through job references) that might be construed as damaging to his or her professional reputation.

- Document the terms of the employee's dismissal.

You or your company's human resource department can address this last point through what's called a separation letter. This letter is addressed to the employee and delivered to him or her during an exit interview. The letter should clarify when the worker's employment ended. Depending on the circumstances of the situation, it may also describe other information:

- Severance benefits, including what kinds and when they will be provided

- Final pay, including any bonuses due and accrued benefits, such as vacation time

- Health-insurance coverage or conversion (e.g., COBRA in the United States)

- Outplacement help

- Treatment of vested stock options

- Any noncompete or nondisclosure agreements

- Any terms stipulated in a collective bargaining agreement

- Any agreements you've made about providing the person with a service letter or references

- Any release the worker has agreed to, such as a promise not to sue the company in exchange for special benefits, such as additional money

In the United States, if the dismissed employee is in what's known as a protected class—such as a minority, disabled, female, or older worker—and he or she has agreed to sign a release, laws regarding the acceptance of the separation letter become more complicated. In this case, you or your company should consult legal counsel regarding exactly how to word the separation letter.

Make No Negative Statements

Once the dismissed employee has left the company, take care not to do or say anything—even in an offhand way—that anyone could perceive as damaging to the former employee's reputation or chances of finding another job. Such a statement could come back to haunt you in the form of a defamation suit or through resentment among the former employee's fellow workers. The best policy is simply not to say anything negative about a former employee.

What About References?

At some point, potential employers of the dismissed individual may phone you or your company as part of their reference-checking process. If the former employee asks you for a reference and you feel you have little or nothing good to say about the person, stick to the bare essentials. Indeed, your company may have a clear policy specifying what information you can provide in a reference. Check with your human resource and legal departments to familiarize yourself with your company's references policies.

A Special Note About Discrimination

Various countries have established laws against dismissing employees on the basis of race, gender, sexual orientation, marital status, physical or mental disability, age, and reproductive status (i.e., whether they're pregnant or plan to become pregnant). Staying on the right side of these laws can sometimes be tricky, which explains why discrimination is the most cited reason for wrongful-discharge claims. So, pay scrupulous attention to how employment discrimination is defined in your situation before deciding whether to dismiss someone. Consulting an experienced lawyer who specializes in employment law is the best way to ensure that you don't unwittingly discriminate against a worker by dismissing him or her.

Notes

Chapter 1

1. Admiral Chester Nimitz, communiqué to Admiral Ray Spruance, quoted in Samuel Eliot Morison, *History of the United States Naval Operation in World War II* (Boston: Little, Brown, 1950), 4:84.

2. Haig R. Nalbantian et al., *Play to Your Strengths: Managing Your Internal Labor Markets for Lasting Competitive Advantage* (New York: McGraw-Hill, 2004), 17–29.

Chapter 2

1. Douglas McGregor, *The Human Side of Management: 25th Anniversary Edition* (New York: McGraw Hill/Irwin, 1985).

2. David A. Garvin and Norman Klein, "A Note on High-Commitment Work Systems," Case 9-693080 (Boston: Harvard Business School, 1993), 2.

3. Linda Hill, *Becoming a Manager* (Boston: Harvard Business School Press, 1992), 72.

4. Brian J. Hall, "Incentive Strategy Within Organizations," Note 9-902-131 (Boston: Harvard Business School, 2002), 1.

5. Frederick Herzberg, "One More Time: How Do You Motivate Employees?" (HBR Classic), *Harvard Business Review*, January 2003, 109–120.

6. Brian J. Hall, "Incentive Strategy Within Organizations," Note 9-902-131 (Boston: Harvard Business School, 2002), 10.

7. Ibid., 13.

8. Timothy Butler and James Waldroop, "Job Sculpting: The Art of Retaining Your Best People," *Harvard Business Review*, September–October 1999, 144–152.

9. Amy C. Edmondson, "Safe to Say at Prudential Financial," Note 5-604-021 (Boston: Harvard Business School, 2004).

10. Gordon Bethune, *From Worst to Best* (New York: John Wiley and Sons, 1998), 36–38.

11. Marcus Buckingham and Curt Coffman, *First, Break All the Rules* (New York: Simon and Schuster, 1999), 34.

Chapter 3

1. John J. Gabarro and Linda Hill, "Managing Performance," Note 9-496-022 (Boston: Harvard Business School, 2002).

Chapter 4

1. This section is adapted from Harvard ManageMentor on Giving and Receiving Feedback, an online product of Harvard Business School Publishing.

2. This section is adapted from Harvard ManageMentor on Coaching, an online product of Harvard Business School Publishing.

Chapter 5

1. J. Richard Hackman, *Leading Teams* (Boston: Harvard Business School Press, 2002), 205.

Chapter 6

1. Dick Grote, "Performance Appraisal Reappraised," *Harvard Business Review*, January 2000, 21.

Chapter 7

1. Clair Brown and Michael Reich, "Developing Skills Through Career Ladders: Lessons from Japanese and U.S. Companies," *California Management Review* 39, no. 2 (1997): 124–125.

2. "Corporate Universities: The New Pioneers of Management Education, An Interview with Jeanne Meister," *Harvard Management Update,* October 1998, 2–4.

Chapter 8

1. Beth Axelrod, Helen Handfield-Jones, and Ed Michaels, "A New Game Plan for C Players," *Harvard Business Review,* January 2002, 82.

Glossary

ACTION PLAN With respect to coaching, a clear statement of goals and the measures of success, a timetable, and a clear indication of how the coach and the coachee will work together.

BURNOUT Work exhaustion, usually from overwork or frustration with jobs that never reach a satisfactory conclusion.

CAREER DEVELOPMENT The many training experiences, work assignments, and mentoring relationships that move people ahead in their vocations.

CAREER LADDER A logical series of stages that move a talented and dedicated employee through progressively more challenging and responsible positions.

CLOSED QUESTIONS Questions that lead to yes or no answers.

COACHING An interactive process through which managers and supervisors aim to accomplish one of two things: (1) to solve performance problems or (2) to develop employee capabilities. The process relies on collaboration and is based on three components: technical help, personal support, and individual challenge.

DELEGATION The assignment of a specific task or project by one person to another.

DIRECT COACHING A coaching style that is most helpful when a coach is working with people who are inexperienced or whose performance requires immediate improvement.

EXTRINSIC REWARDS Rewards that are external, tangible forms of recognition such as pay hikes, promotions, bonuses, and sales prizes.

HAWTHORNE EFFECT The productivity benefits that a company creates when it pays attention to its employees and treats them as something other than mere cogs in the machinery of production.

INTRINSIC REWARDS Rewards that produce nonquantifiable personal satisfaction, such as a sense of accomplishment, personal control over one's work, and a feeling that one's work is appreciated.

OPEN-ENDED QUESTIONS Questions that invite participation and idea sharing.

PERFORMANCE APPRAISAL A formal method for assessing how well people are doing with respect to their assigned goals. Its ultimate purpose is to communicate personal goals, to encourage good performance, to provide feedback, and to correct poor performance.

PERFORMANCE GAP The difference between a subordinate's current performance and what is required by the job—or by the job you'd like the subordinate to take on.

PERFORMANCE MANAGEMENT A method used to measure and improve the effectiveness of people in the workplace.

SKILL DEFICIENCY A gap between a person's current capabilities and those needed to take on another job.

SUPPORTIVE COACHING A coaching style in which the coach acts as a facilitator or guide.

360-DEGREE FEEDBACK A personal assessment tool used to systematically collect information about a person's behavior and performance from key people who interact with that person: boss, peers, and direct reports. The goal is to determine what it is like working for or with the person, and to isolate strengths and weaknesses.

For Further Reading

Appraisal

Carney, Karen. "Successful Performance Measurement: A Checklist." *Harvard Management Update*, November 1999. Does your performance measurement system actually boost performance? Here's a checklist for ensuring meaningful performance measurement. The article includes an annotated "If You Want to Learn More" section and a sidebar, "Measuring the Soft Stuff," which addresses soft metrics.

Coens, Tom, and Mary Jenkins. *Abolishing Performance Appraisals: Why They Backfire and What They Do Instead.* San Francisco: Berrett-Koehler, 2000. There are plenty of books and articles on performance appraisals and how to make them more effective. This book articulates the case against appraisals, asserting that they are not only annoying but counterproductive. In their place, the authors suggest alternatives to the purposes of appraisals—valid and necessary purposes such as coaching, feedback, pay and promotion decisions, and the documentation of employee performance. So, if you'd like to dump the performance appraisal but are fearful of abandoning its purposes, look here for practical ideas.

Grote, Dick. *The Performance Appraisal Question and Answer Book.* New York: Amacom, 2002. If done correctly, says the author, a performance appraisal can be one of the valuable tools available to managers. Using a Q&A format, Grote, a former manager at General Electric and PepsiCo, focuses on practical details. This is a good guide to getting it right.

Harvard Business School Publishing. "Alternatives to the Annual Performance Review." *Harvard Management Update,* February 2000. Companies can get rid of those troublesome yearly evaluations if they really want to. But it isn't an easy move to make. Managers have to change

141

some fundamental assumptions about what really produces high performance. And companies have to work with employees differently on a variety of fronts, from feedback to compensation.

Johnson, Lauren Keller. "The Ratings Game: Retooling 360s for Better Performance." *Harvard Management Update,* January 2004. After earning its stripes in professional development, the 360-degree feedback tool has insinuated itself into the performance appraisal processes at an increasing number of companies. But the colleague-based feedback that has made the 360 such a favored tool in development can be its Achilles' heel in performance reviews: Most people possess a deep ambivalence about wielding power over a peer's livelihood. Read about how people are reshaping the tool so that it not only encourages direct and honest feedback in annual reviews, but also fits the particular needs and priorities of a broad range of organizations.

McGregor, Douglas. "An Uneasy Look at Performance Appraisal." *Harvard Business Review,* September–October 1972. Not everyone has been happy with the widely used tool of performance appraisal—not now, and not then. In this classic article, the father of Theory Y notes his ambivalence. In his view, the conventional approach to performance appraisal forces managers to make judgments on the personal worth of a fellow employee. He believes that an effective alternative is employee self-evaluation. This requires that employees think about their jobs, assess carefully their own strengths and weaknesses, and formulate specific plans to reach their goals. The boss's role is to help correlate the employee's self-appraisal goals and plans with the concerns of the organization. This system places the major responsibility on the subordinate and shifts the emphasis from appraisal to analysis.

Coaching

Waldroop, James, and Timothy Butler. "The Executive As Coach." *Harvard Business Review*, OnPoint Enhanced Edition, November 2000. How do you deal with the talented manager whose perfectionism paralyzes his or her direct reports or the high-performing expert who disdains teamwork? What about the sensitive manager who avoids confrontation of any kind? Get rid of these people? The authors suggest that you coach them. Helping to change the behaviors that threaten to derail a valued manager is often the best way to help that manager succeed. Executives increasingly recognize that people-management skills are the key to both their personal success and the success of their business. And being an effective coach is a crucial part of successful people management.

Delegating

Schwartz, Andrew E. *Delegating Authority.* New York: Barron's Business Success Series, 1992. Delegating is an effective way to develop the skills of subordinates. It demonstrates trust on your part and gives the subordinate an opportunity to rise to a new challenge. This handy pocket guide to delegation provides both new and experienced managers with an overview of the essential skills and techniques needed to delegate effectively. It discusses delegation in terms of five key components: goal setting, communication, motivation, supervision, and evaluation. There are recommendations for specific techniques and approaches within each component.

General

Hill, Linda. *Becoming a Manager: Mastery of a New Identity.* 2nd ed. Boston: Harvard Business School Press, 2003. The transition from individual contributor to manager can be trying—even traumatic—for many people. Hill traces the experiences of nineteen new managers to unravel the complexity of the process. As these personal interviews reveal, becoming a manager represents a profound psychological transformation—one that all-too-many individuals fail to make. Hill provides concrete, practical suggestions for companies to help managers survive their first year and become major contributors to their organizations.

Goals

Covey, Stephen R., A. Roger Merrill, and Rebecca R. Merrill. *First Things First: To Live, to Love, and to Leave a Legacy.* New York: Simon and Schuster, 1995. A good source for anyone trying to define goals. The authors emphasize analyzing balance to achieve more in your personal and professional life. With a series of scenarios and exercises, the book explores how to define true goals and achieve them by looking at what motivates you.

Smith, Douglas K. *Make Success Measurable!* New York: John Wiley and Sons, 1999. This book shows how to avoid activity-based goals that can go on indefinitely and how to articulate aggressive, outcome-based goals that are specific, measurable, achievable, relevant, and time-bound. This is a how-to book, emphasizing outcomes as opposed to actions in setting goals. Lessons include how to set goals that matter to customers, shareholders, and funders; how to set nonfinancial as well as financial goals and link them; how to understand and use outcome-based goals that support success while avoiding activity-based goals that produce failure; and how to select and use management disciplines needed to achieve your goals.

Straub, Joseph T. "Setting Goals and Planning." In *The Successful New Manager.* New York: AMACOM, 1994. The author discusses how to involve your direct reports in the goal-setting process. He identifies obstacles to achieving goals and details how to address each one.

Motivation

Herzberg, Frederick. "One More Time: How Do You Motivate Employees?" *Harvard Business Review,* January 2003. This is a classic of management literature. The psychology of motivation is very complex, but the surest way of getting someone to do something is to deliver a kick in the pants—put bluntly, the KITA. Companies usually resort to positive KITAs, which range from fringe benefits to employee counseling. But although a KITA might produce some change in behavior, it doesn't motivate. Frederick Herzberg, whose work influenced a generation of scholars and managers, likens motivation to an internal generator. An employee with an internal generator, he argues, needs no KITA. Achievement, recognition for achievement, the work itself, responsibility, and growth or advancement motivate people. The author cites research showing that those intrinsic factors are distinct from extrinsic, or KITA, elements that lead to job dissatisfaction. Jobs can be changed and enriched. Managers should focus on positions in which people's attitudes are poor. The investment needed in industrial engineering is cost effective, and motivation will make a difference in performance.

Livingston, J. Sterling. "Pygmalion in Management." *Harvard Business Review,* January 2003. What has long been recognized by teachers, physicians, and behavioral scientists holds true for management: one person's expectations shape another person's behavior. If a manager has high expectations, employees are likely to excel; if expectations are low, employees will probably respond with poor performance. In this classic *Harvard Business Review* article from 1969, J. Sterling Livingston draws on numerous case studies and other research to demonstrate the importance of managerial expectations in individual and group performance. Consider the insurance executive who identified his six best agents and assigned them to his most capable manager. Not surprisingly, this group surpassed its already ambitious target. Equally unsurprising was what happened to a group of low producers assigned to the company's least capable manager. Their performance declined even further. But what happened to the group of average agents assigned to an average manager? That group increased its productivity by a higher percentage than the top group, because the manager refused to consider herself—or her agents—less capable than the superstars. And managers' beliefs about themselves influence how they view and treat their employees.

Maslow, Abraham. *Motivation and Personality.* New York: Harper Collins, 1987. Psychologist Abraham Maslow published his famous Hierarchy of Needs in the original 1954 edition of this book. It was last revised in 1970. In Maslow's hierarchy, people first must satisfy basic needs before they are motivated to satisfy others. In this ascending order of need, physiological needs come first (food, shelter). Security needs (protection from danger) come next, followed by social needs (love, friendship, comradeship) and ego needs (self-respect, sense of self-worth). Once these needs are satisfied, the person can move on to self-actualization—a sense of realizing his or her full potential. Maslow's hierarchy remains a potent and useful basis for understanding human behavior and motivation.

McGregor, Douglas. *The Human Side of Enterprise.* Annotated edition. New York: McGraw-Hill/Irwin, 2006. Few books can approach the influence that this one has had on the field of management. First published in 1960, this book indelibly stamped the field of management with McGregor's now famous Theory X and Theory Y perceptions of human nature in the workplace. This annotated edition contains suggestions on how today's managers can put his management concepts to work.

Morse, John J., and Jay W. Lorsch. "Beyond Theory Y." *Harvard Business Review*, May 1970. Douglas McGregor's Theory Y fails to explain worker motivation under all circumstances. Recent studies show that there is no single best organizational approach, and that the best approach is one fitted to the nature of the work to be done. Contingency theory states that an individual's central need is to achieve a sense of competence. Competence is most likely to be fulfilled when there is a fit between the task and the organization. In this situation, competence continues after the achievement of initial goals.

Problem Employees

Delpo, Amy, and Lisa Guerin. *Dealing with Problem Employees: A Legal Guide.* Berkeley, CA: Nolo, 2001. Problem employees pose an enormous number of legal and other challenges. This book shows you how to recognize who is and who isn't a problem employee, help problem employees get back on track, investigate problems and complaints, conduct effective performance evaluations, apply progressive discipline, and handle the many complex aspects of dismissals.

Gosset, Steve. "Sometimes You Do Have to Fire People." *Harvard Management Communications Letter*, October 1999. Dismissing an employee for cause can be the beginning of more headaches if you're not careful, according to this article. As told here, a sales manager was the subject of sexual harassment complaints in four different offices. The company wasted no time conducting a thorough investigation and found overwhelming evidence against the manager. He was called in by the company president to be fired. But the president was too embarrassed to discuss the real reason for the termination and blurted out, "Bernie, we think it's time you retire." The boss may have believed he was giving the manager a graceful way out of the company. He was wrong. Instead of doing the right thing for the principal reason, he now found himself on the wrong end of an age discrimination complaint, which cost his company a lot of money. The article sums up its tips about firing with "The Ten Commandments of Termination."

Nicholson, Nigel, "How Do You Motivate Your Problem People?" *Harvard Business Review*, January 2003. Managers who motivate with incentives and the power of their vision and passion succeed only in energizing employees who want to be motivated. So, how do you motivate intractable employees—the ones who never do what you want and also take up all your time? According to Nigel Nicholson, you can't; individuals must motivate themselves. Instead of pushing solutions on problem employees, the manager should pull solutions out of them by creating circumstances in which the employees can channel their motivation toward achievable goals. That means addressing any obstacles—possibly even the manager's own demotivating style—that might be hindering the employees. Using detailed examples, Nicholson walks the reader through his method, pointing out potential pitfalls along the way. First, the manager creates a rich picture of the problem person. Second, the manager exercises flexibility and reframes goals so that the employee can meet them. Third, in a carefully staged, face-to-face conversation, the manager meets with the problem employee on neutral ground.

Weeks, Holly. "Taking the Stress Out of Stressful Conversations." *Harvard Business Review*, OnPoint Enhanced Edition, March 2002. Dismissing an employee can be one of the most stressful conversations a manager can face. That's because such conversations are emotionally loaded. Weeks explains the emotional dynamics that take place in stressful conversations and emphasizes the importance of preparation before delivering painful news to an employee. She describes a method for identifying your vulnerabilities during stressful conversations and practicing delivery styles and behaviors that are more effective.

Index

About the Subject Adviser

BRIAN J. HALL is a Professor of Business Administration at Harvard Business School, where he is a member of the Negotiation, Organizations and Markets Unit and a faculty affiliate of the Rock Center for Entrepreneurship. Previously, he was an assistant professor of economics in the Harvard Economics Department. Professor Hall received his BA, MA, and PhD in economics from Harvard University and holds an MPhil in economics from Cambridge University. He was on the staff of the President's Council of Economics Advisers in 1990–1991.

Professor Hall teaches and conducts research in the area of organizational strategy, with a focus on performance management and incentive systems. He teaches a second-year elective course called Coordination, Control and the Management of Organizations: Incentives (CCMO) in the Harvard MBA program, as well as various modules and courses in the Harvard Business School's executive education programs.

Professor Hall's research has been published in a variety of academic and practitioner-oriented journals, including the *American Economic Review*, the *Quarterly Journal of Economics*, and the *Harvard Business Review*. He has also written numerous cases in the area of organizational strategy, performance management, corporate governance, and incentives. His research is frequently in the national and international financial press, and he has been the featured speaker at numerous conferences and symposia. He has provided expert testimony before the U.S. Senate and appeared on CNBC and *NewsHour* with Jim Lehrer.

Professor Hall is a Faculty Research Fellow at the National Bureau of Economic Research and has been a part of the Global Corporate Governance and Human Resource Initiatives at the Harvard Business School. He has served as a consultant and an adviser to many leading international companies in a variety of sectors. He is currently on leave as Executive Vice President of Alghanim Industries, one of the largest multibusiness companies in the Middle East, with over five thousand employees in thirty countries.

About the Writer

RICHARD LUECKE is the writer of this and other books in the Harvard Business Essentials series. Based in Salem, Massachusetts, Mr. Luecke has authored or developed over forty books, dozens of articles, and several training courses on a wide range of business subjects. He has an MBA from the University of St. Thomas. He can be reached at richard.luecke@verizon.net.

Harvard Business Review Paperback Series

The Harvard Business Review Paperback Series offers the best thinking on cutting-edge management ideas from the world's leading thinkers, researchers, and managers. Designed for leaders who believe in the power of ideas to change business, these books will be useful to managers at all levels of experience, but especially senior executives and general managers. In addition, this series is widely used in training and executive development programs.

Books are priced at $19.95 U.S.
Price subject to change.

Title	Product #
Harvard Business Review **Interviews with CEOs**	3294
Harvard Business Review on **Advances in Strategy**	8032
Harvard Business Review on **Appraising Employee Performance**	7685
Harvard Business Review on **Becoming a High Performance Manager**	1296
Harvard Business Review on **Brand Management**	1445
Harvard Business Review on **Breakthrough Leadership**	8059
Harvard Business Review on **Breakthrough Thinking**	181X
Harvard Business Review on **Building Personal and Organizational Resilience**	2721
Harvard Business Review on **Business and the Environment**	2336
Harvard Business Review on **The Business Value of IT**	9121
Harvard Business Review on **Change**	8842
Harvard Business Review on **Compensation**	701X
Harvard Business Review on **Corporate Ethics**	273X
Harvard Business Review on **Corporate Governance**	2379
Harvard Business Review on **Corporate Responsibility**	2748
Harvard Business Review on **Corporate Strategy**	1429
Harvard Business Review on **Crisis Management**	2352
Harvard Business Review on **Culture and Change**	8369
Harvard Business Review on **Customer Relationship Management**	6994

Title	Product #
Harvard Business Review on **Decision Making**	5572
Harvard Business Review on **Developing Leaders**	5003
Harvard Business Review on **Doing Business in China**	6387
Harvard Business Review on **Effective Communication**	1437
Harvard Business Review on **Entrepreneurship**	9105
Harvard Business Review on **Finding and Keeping the Best People**	5564
Harvard Business Review on **Innovation**	6145
Harvard Business Review on **The Innovative Enterprise**	130X
Harvard Business Review on **Knowledge Management**	8818
Harvard Business Review on **Leadership**	8834
Harvard Business Review on **Leadership at the Top**	2756
Harvard Business Review on **Leadership in a Changed World**	5011
Harvard Business Review on **Leading in Turbulent Times**	1806
Harvard Business Review on **Managing Diversity**	7001
Harvard Business Review on **Managing High-Tech Industries**	1828
Harvard Business Review on **Managing People**	9075
Harvard Business Review on **Managing Projects**	6395
Harvard Business Review on **Managing the Value Chain**	2344
Harvard Business Review on **Managing Uncertainty**	9083
Harvard Business Review on **Managing Your Career**	1318
Harvard Business Review on **Marketing**	8040
Harvard Business Review on **Measuring Corporate Performance**	8826
Harvard Business Review on **Mergers and Acquisitions**	5556
Harvard Business Review on **Mind of the Leader**	6409
Harvard Business Review on **Motivating People**	1326
Harvard Business Review on **Negotiation**	2360
Harvard Business Review on **Nonprofits**	9091
Harvard Business Review on **Organizational Learning**	6153
Harvard Business Review on **Strategic Alliances**	1334
Harvard Business Review on **Strategies for Growth**	8850
Harvard Business Review on **Teams That Succeed**	502X
Harvard Business Review on **Turnarounds**	6366
Harvard Business Review on **What Makes a Leader**	6374
Harvard Business Review on **Work and Life Balance**	3286

To order, call 1-800-668-6780, or go online at www.HBSPress.org

Management Dilemmas: Case Studies from the Pages of Harvard Business Review

When facing a difficult management challenge, wouldn't it be great if you could turn to a panel of experts to help guide you to the right decision? Now you can, with books from the Management Dilemmas series. Drawn from the pages of *Harvard Business Review,* each insightful guide poses a range of familiar and perplexing business situations and shares the wisdom of a small group of leading experts on how each of them would resolve the problem. Engagingly written, these interactive, solutions-oriented collections allow readers to match wits with the experts. They are designed to help managers hone their instincts and problem-solving skills to make sound judgment calls on everyday management dilemmas.

These books are priced at $19.95 U.S.
Price subject to change.

Title	Product #
Management Dilemmas: **When Change Comes Undone**	5038
Management Dilemmas: **When Good People Behave Badly**	5046
Management Dilemmas: **When Marketing Becomes a Minefield**	290X
Management Dilemmas: **When People Are the Problem**	7138
Management Dilemmas: **When Your Strategy Stalls**	712X

To order, call 1-800-668-6780, or go online at www.HBSPress.org

Harvard Business Essentials

In the fast-paced world of business today, everyone needs a personal resource—a place to go for advice, coaching, background information, or answers. The Harvard Business Essentials series fits the bill. Concise and straightforward, these books provide highly practical advice for readers at all levels of experience. Whether you are a new manager interested in expanding your skills or an experienced executive looking to stay on top, these solution-oriented books give you the reliable tips and tools you need to improve your performance and get the job done. Harvard Business Essentials titles will quickly become your constant companions and trusted guides.

These books are priced at $19.95 U.S., except as noted.
Price subject to change.

Title	Product #
Harvard Business Essentials: **Negotiation**	1113
Harvard Business Essentials: **Managing Creativity and Innovation**	1121
Harvard Business Essentials: **Managing Change and Transition**	8741
Harvard Business Essentials: **Hiring and Keeping the Best People**	875X
Harvard Business Essentials: **Finance for Managers**	8768
Harvard Business Essentials: **Business Communication**	113X
Harvard Business Essentials: **Manager's Toolkit ($24.95)**	2896
Harvard Business Essentials: **Managing Projects Large and Small**	3213
Harvard Business Essentials: **Creating Teams with an Edge**	290X
Harvard Business Essentials: **Entrepreneur's Toolkit**	4368
Harvard Business Essentials: **Coaching and Mentoring**	435X
Harvard Business Essentials: **Crisis Management**	4376
Harvard Business Essentials: **Time Management**	6336
Harvard Business Essentials: **Power, Influence, and Persuasion**	631X
Harvard Business Essentials: **Strategy**	6328
Harvard Business Essentials: **Decision Making**	7618
Harvard Business Essentials: **Marketer's Toolkit**	7626

To order, call 1-800-668-6780, or go online at www.HBSPress.org

The Results-Driven Manager

The Results-Driven Manager series collects timely articles from Harvard Management Update and Harvard Management Communication Letter to help senior to middle managers sharpen their skills, increase their effectiveness, and gain a competitive edge. Presented in a concise, accessible format to save managers valuable time, these books offer authoritative insights and techniques for improving job performance and achieving immediate results.

These books are priced at $14.95 U.S.
Price subject to change.

How to Order

Harvard Business School Press publications are available worldwide from your local bookseller or online retailer.
You can also call

1-800-668-6780

Our product consultants are available to help you
8:00 a.m.–6:00 p.m., Monday–Friday, Eastern Time.
Outside the U.S. and Canada, call: 617-783-7450
Please call about special discounts for quantities greater than ten.

You can order online at

www.HBSPress.org